MADE IN ABINGDON

Echoes from the shopfloor

Bob Frampton

www.veloce.co.uk

First published in March 2018 by Veloce Publishing Limited, Veloce House, Parkway Farm Business Park, Middle Farm Way, Poundbury, Dorchester DT1 3AR, England. Tel +44 (0)1305 260068 / Fax 01305 250479 / e-mail info@veloce.co.uk / web www.veloce.co.uk or www.velocebooks.com. Reprinted October 2019.
ISBN: 978-1-787112-68-1; UPC: 6-36847-01268-7.

MADE IN ABINGDON

Echoes from the shopfloor

Bob Frampton

VELOCE

For Claire and Mary Frampton

Also by Bob Frampton:

Abingdon in the Great War
The Abingdon Races
Abingdon and The Boer War
The Cinemas of Abingdon
Abingdon in the Second World War

Contents

Introduction

The MG Car Company, known to many as simply 'The Gs', and rarely as 'MGs', relocated from Oxford to Abingdon in 1929, moving into surplus Pavlova Leather Company buildings situated between Marcham Road and Cemetery Road. In the beginning these buildings still contained piles of wool and leather goods, and were like a 'wool loft' according to one ex-employee.

The company prospered, manufacturing mainly sports cars, and entered a number of motorsport competitions in the Thirties, with considerable success; among them, Monte Carlo, the 1930 Double Twelve at Brooklands, the Land's End Trial and the Le Mans 24-hour race.

The development of high-performance cars was interrupted by the Second World War, when the company acquired government contracts to build or develop a wide range of military material, ranging from armoured fighting vehicles, American trucks, Albemarle aircraft noses, wing parts for Tempest and Typhoon aircraft, Lancaster bomber engines and much more. It even constructed blood centrifuge equipment for the Admiralty.

In 1955, the BMC (British Motor Corporation) Competition Department was set up in Cowley, Oxford, with Brian Moylan on the team, making adaptations to bring Minis up to a level to compete in such rallies as Monte Carlo, Le Mans, the 1970 London to Mexico World Cup Rally, and the London to Sydney Marathon. Brian and others have written extensively about events in this period.

1979 was the Golden Jubilee of the company in Abingdon, and was marked by a big celebration that included sports events, a hot-air balloon, floats and much more. However, very soon afterwards the company was closed down.

The passages which follow in this book result from a series of interviews, often in the form of notes, and are written with the aim of recording some of the thoughts and experiences of the people who worked in the company, from the war period up to the final closure.

In its 50 years in Abingdon there were, it is claimed, very few strikes, while no other part of the British Motor Corporation or British Leyland could make a similar claim. How accurate is this?

The same memories and experiences were, of course, often shared by a number of people, so some recollections appear more than once. One regret is that this book was not written years earlier, as we now have too few reminiscences of those early prewar years.

I thank all my contributors, and apologise now if they find that the events they related to me have become altered slightly. This is a result of inaccuracies in both my note-taking and my memory. I am also very aware that almost everyone reading this will know far more than I do about the whole MG operation.

In its history the company experienced several changes of ownership: after being founded by Sir William Morris, it became successively Morris Motors Limited, British Motor Corporation, British Motor Holdings, and finally British Leyland. Despite this, the loyalty of the workforce seems to have been always with MG, rather than one or other of these corporate entities. One point comes across very strongly: people were proud to work there, very happy to work with a successful and forward-looking company, which they felt, treated them well.

As the years pass, their feelings have not changed.

Bob Frampton
Abingdon

NEW INDUSTRY FOR ABINGDON
MG Car Co. Acquires Big Factory
FIVE-ACRE SITE

The acquisition of a large factory at Abingdon marks another stage in the rapid growth of the MG Car Co, the enterprising Oxford firm of car manufacturers, and is also of importance to Abingdon itself from the industrial point of view.

Starting in 1925 with one small workshop in Pusey Lane, Oxford, with a frontage of 20 feet and a depth of 100 feet, the MG Co. soon found the demand for their product increasing so rapidly that they moved to a small factory at Bainton Road.

Progress was still so rapid that within two years they were obliged to build a factory at Cowley costing £20,000 and occupying about 80,360 square feet of floor space. At these works the MG Sports Cars have been manufactured for just over two years and now the demand has become so great that it has again been found necessary to find much larger premises.

The New Works

These have been secured in the factory adjoining The Pavlova Leather Co's present works at Abingdon and covering an effective area of about five acres and this vast space will shortly be humming with the activity of the MG Car Co the whole of whose production is to be transferred there from Cowley.

It is hoped to employ about 200 people at the Abingdon works for a start, and as far as possible local labour will be used, but it goes without saying that the heads of departments and skilled men will have to be transferred from Cowley.

Separate Organisation

Although the MG Sports Car is produced under the aegis of Sir William Morris, one must not associate it in any way with either the Morris Oxford or the Morris Cowley. The whole organisation of the MG Car Co. is entirely separate and their products, especially the MG Six Sports, bear little, if any, resemblance to any of the other products of Cowley.

The fact that the MG's specification is of the best (no consideration of cost being allowed to stand in the way) and the individual attention each car receives, account largely for the way in which the car has come to be recognised so soon as ranking amongst the world's finest Sports Cars combining refinement and distinctive appearance with remarkable performance at a moderate figure.

THE CAR BL CAN'T AFFORD TO SELL

MG car production at Abingdon is to cease under BL's latest survival plan. The historic MG Company, which has just celebrated its Golden Jubilee, is no longer a winner. It has become a casualty of the high rate of exchange.

The falling value of the dollar and the rising value of the pound have reduced the profit margin on MG cars sold in the United States.

For nearly 30 years the West Coast has been the best market for the Abingdon sports cars; 80 per cent are exported, and 70 per cent go to America.

Over the years they have earned literally millions of dollars for Britain, but because of the high rate of exchange, exporting them has ceased to be profitable. "Our sales price in the U.S. does not give us sufficient return to justify production," says BL.

It was a cruel irony that half the workers on the MGB lines were laid off when the news broke on Monday.

About 450 men were laid off until today because of a parts shortage caused by the engineering strike, which the Abingdon workers have chosen to ignore. It was their second period of lay-off – without pay – because of the national dispute, which created a shortage of axles.

The MG Works has what has often claimed to be the best labour relations in the whole of British Leyland: the time lost through internal disputes has been infinitesimal compared with that in other car plants.

The news that car production is to cease came just after the climax of the company's Golden Jubilee celebrations.

In Abingdon on Saturday they were toasting the next 50 years; no one really believed that the toast would turn hollow within two days.

9

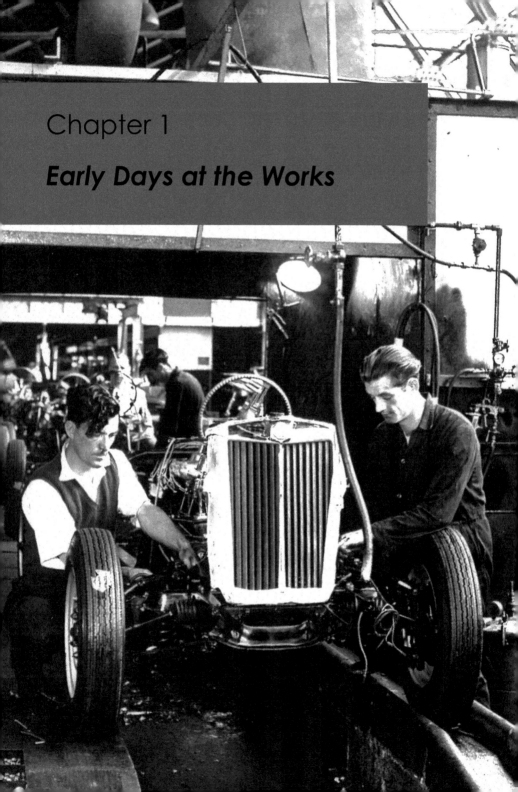

Chapter 1

Early Days at the Works

Time Passes

It's a sad fact that we have few personal reminiscences from the early days of MG, but those that we do have are interesting in themselves. In 1929 MG came to Abingdon, after it had begun life in Oxford as a sideline for Morris Garages General Manager, Cecil Kimber, known to many as 'CK.' Such was its success as a marque that, in that year, the MG Car Company was born.

The period before the Second World War was a time when one reads of 'Old No 1,' the first MG car, which won a Gold Medal in the 1925 Land's End Trial, or the 18/80 Mk II, which took part in the Monte Carlo Rally, and in 1931 won the RAC rally coachwork class. We read of the 'Magic

MG staff and management in 1929.

Back row, left to right: R Hewson, V Vines, C Haddock, J Craigmile, H Robinson, J Clewley, J Reed, Snr, W Smith, S Enever, P L Watson, H G Cox, H D Jones, S Good, P Hughes, W Higgs, J Lewis, R F Howse. **Middle row, left to right:** *J Hunt, J R Pennock, J Lewis, R C Jackson, C Martin, G Denton, J Bull, G King, G Phillips, M Prickett, F Stevens, B L Calcutt, J Lowndes, M Wakelin, M O McLennan, H M Rummins, C Nash, H Herring, L Shurrock, G Morris, P Kent.* **Front row, left to right:** *C Cousins, A W Lepine, R A Maynard, G Propert, C Kimber, T W Slingsby, J W Thornley, G C Tuck.*

Midget,' the 12/12 M-Type Midget which was a very popular vehicle in the 1930s, and famously driven by Captain George Eyston at 120mph in 1932.

1931 – Flannel Dance

Back at Abingdon and away from most of the glamour of competition, it was not all work.

While in many sectors of the UK economy the Thirties was perceived as a period of gloom, MG contributed to and brought prosperity to Abingdon in many ways. On Friday 15th of May 1931, the *North Berks Herald* carried a notice announcing that the management of the MG Social Club on Ock Street, in the Beaconsfield Building to the left of the Clock House, was holding a 'Flannel Dance' at the Corn Exchange, Abingdon, from 8pm until 2am.

Although the MG Social Club was a two-storey block, with a full-size billiards table upstairs, and a bar (beer 3½d a pint), darts, and so on downstairs, it was clearly not large enough to accommodate a dance-floor and band.

'Flannel dances' were informal balls, where those attending could wear open-necked shirts and jackets, and flannel trousers. This was in contrast to the normal dance, where formal attire would be expected.

Presumably it was open to the general public. Music would be provided by Jack Viner's Band, and there would be a bar. Tickets were obtainable from MG at 2/6d, and buses would return people to Oxford after the dance.

The Sports Club later moved to West Saint Helen Street on the site of the old Clarke's factory, and in the 1960s to a purpose-built site on Caldecott Road.

Frank 'Dutchy' Holland

Dutchy, who lived in Exbourne Road, Abingdon, began at the company as a tea-boy, as did many others. 60 years or so later he wrote *My Life*, an interesting description of the Works and some of its employees (as yet, unpublished). Of course, some of the departments described would have changed location over the years.

He began work at MG in 1935 in the Dispatch Department with Jack Sparrow, and his first wages were three shillings and a half-penny for a 44-hour week.

For his first day's work he purchased a set of overalls from Beesley's in the High Street. He was required to fetch tea and a Chelsea bun for each worker twice a day from the canteen, and then work on the completed cars lined up in neat rows in the Dispatch area. Each car was fitted with a small roll of tools, including a copper hammer for hubcaps, spanners, screwdrivers and so on. The cars were 'P' types or 'N' types.

On one occasion, Sir John Fry of Fry's Chocolate arrived, complete with staff and a chauffeur. For helping out with Fry's arrangements for collecting a car, Dutchy was given a silver three-penny piece.

In those days Dispatch was found along Marcham Road. New cars were ready for collection from there, and collected by 'trade-plate men'. These plates were temporarily attached to a motor vehicle by a motor trader before proper registration had taken place. Agents would be sent by dealers from all over the country, who made their way to Abingdon and then drove the cars back. An 'N-type' cost about £365, whereas, for comparison, a new house in Thesiger Road or Abbott Road cost £375.

In the early days, if you applied for a job at MG, the application form stated that you had to bring in with you any tools you had. One applicant, Horace Carter, was Cecil Kimber's gardener who wanted to better himself, so went for a job as an assembler on the Chassis Line. As the form requested, Horace brought his own tools with him – spade, hoe, fork and rake.

Dutchy's Tour
Beginning the tour on the left of the Works entrance, a wall separated Dispatch from Service Repair, and to the east was Service Stores with Bill Smith, Eddie Dixon, Bill Steptoe and George Jeffries, to name a few. Moving towards Cemetery Road, there was the Body Deck above the Body Assembly Line, with John Bull the foreman, 'Maggie' Buckle, Arthur Belcher, and tea-boys Percy Hudson and Les Morse. Much trimming was carried out by such men as Harry Herring, Alf Henson and others.

Going northwards there were the Rectifiers, who corrected any faults revealed after test drives, and also the paint ovens where Cyril Hudson and Frank Stevens worked. Then came the Chassis Line of workers, among whom were Dick Way and Jack Lewis.

At the bottom of the Chassis Line (where the canteen was when the factory finally closed), was Production Stores. Its upper deck contained all the lighter material, such as nuts, bolts, looms and the like, while underneath were the heavier things, such as engines, axles, shockers and chassis frames.

Les Shurrock was the foreman here. All the parts were lowered to the floor in little box trucks, about three feet square and deep, by an electric hoist operated by 'Brassy' Tombs. Among the workers here was Harry Marsh, the first Abingdon man to be killed in action with the local Territorials in the war.

To the right of this was the Tool Store. Bill Gerring and Stan Saunders were to be found here.

Coming back towards Cemetery Road, was the entrance to the Press or Machine Shop, run by George Denton, who was also the landlord of The Crown public house in Ock Street. Three of the men working here were Harry Hudson, George Wiggins and Arthur King. Next came the Tyre Bay, and, close to this, a place known as 'Units' which produced 'one-off' jobs, such as pipe jigs and some experimental work. In here worked Harold Wiggins and Cyril Winter. Cyril was well known for his Harmonica Band consisting of harmonicas, piano accordions and drums. It once played on BBC radio on *The Carol Levis Discoveries Show* and performed twice a week at The Regal Cinema in town.

Next were the offices, near the main Cemetery Road entrance. The building was known to all as 'Top Office'. The Reception, downstairs, was staffed by a man in a chocolate and cream coloured uniform, with 'MG' embroidered on the lapels. Among the ladies that worked upstairs were

Six-cylinder MkIII MGs en route to Coventry, 1927-1929.

Mrs Wiffen, Marjory Prickett, and Miss McLennan, and the men included Les Mott, Jack Read and Reg Ingram.

To the west of the factory was the cinder track near B Block on which testers put each car through its paces. In later years some were tested on the roads.

Dutchy mentions a signalling system inside the Works. On the wall inside the factory, from Cemetery Road to Marcham Road, there was a series of light-bulbs placed high on the walls for communication purposes. The people deemed important enough were allocated a bulb, or combination of two bulbs, and the purpose was to tell them they were wanted on the phone. A klaxon horn would blow (and nearly blow your head off), and you would look at the lights – if your combination was glowing, you would have to get to the nearest phone.

A point he makes is that cars were, at that time, made to order, and people were paid only when a car came off the line. There were no trade

MG TA models on production lines at the Abingdon factory, with MG SA saloon cars in the background.

unions in the prewar period, and unemployment was high generally, so there was little choice but to accept the conditions on offer. Occasionally, when there was a shortage of orders, they would have to attend the Labour Exchange, as it was then called. This was located behind the Town Hall, and men were allotted 4/6d for signing on for three days. Sometimes the men queued four deep, and shuffled around to the dole office for a few shillings, the line stretching from the office then along Lombard Street and into West Saint Helen Street.

Eventually Dutchy was conscripted, and went off to the war, serving with the Royal Artillery in such places as Egypt, Italy and Austria. He served in Malta during the siege of 1942, where he lived for a long time on starvation rations, which affected his health for many years afterwards. He was to return to MG soon after peace returned.

Chapter 2

MG at War

Reorganisation and War Routine

The booklet, *MG War Time Activities*, edited by Colin Grant of the MG Car Club, reveals that in 1939 the management quickly realised that civilian car production would stop, and the factory be given over to war production of some sort. The production equipment was generally removed, leaving space for whatever was to come next. Contracts were sought, and at last work was begun on light tanks, then aircraft, and a great deal of other war work.

One of Dutchy Holland's tasks before conscription was to help fortify the Works with piles of sandbags, and to paint the glass roofs black.

MG Works was one of the larger employers in town, and most families seem to have had someone working there. Some families had several. It was a very close neighbour of the Pavlova Leather Company, and for a time, early in the war, the MG Works and Pavlova shared canteen facilities. To start with, both sets of employees took a lunch break at the same time, but this caused a great crush, so lunch hour became staggered between a 12.30 start and a 13.00 start, and the two companies lunched at different times.

Most of the staff would choose to bicycle to and from work; there was not even a staff car park there. In any event, petrol rationing would have precluded use of cars. Many staff would also cycle home for their main meal of the day at lunchtime. In the evening the normal practice was to have a light meal.

24th May 1940 – War Insurance

The coming of war brought many changes. One of these certainly helped ease the stress of possible attacks and the likely consequences: Lord Nuffield announced that war work would continue on seven days a week, and that, if material for it was available, overtime for day and night shifts would be payable. In another initiative, families of any employee killed or injured by enemy action could claim up to £100 from an insurance scheme set up by Lord Nuffield, though there is no evidence of such a claim actually being made.

'G' (MG Works) Company

The MG factory had its own part of the Home Guard, G (MG Works) Company. For the workforce this meant that, as well as their normal daily work, they had their stint at duty two or three nights a week in the Home Guard and its waterborne section, the Upper Thames Patrol. Some

The fruits of Dutchy Holland's labours apparent in the darkened factory, where Tempest wings were erected in February 1944.

Cycling to work – evidence in the MG factory bike racks in the 1930s.

of these workers would later be called up for regular military service.

G Company at the MG Works comprised 80 members, not all of whom were MG employees. Half were, in fact, employees at Pavlova. Its No 31 Platoon came from Wellworthy, the car piston-ring manufacturer close to MG. Some of the members were: George Warwick, Chris Godfrey, Jack Sparrow, Sam Nash and Reg Turner. The MG Home Guard's main role was officially described as 'anti-sabotage and static defence', ie, guarding factories near the MG Works. After having been drilled by a TA drill-instructor it could produce very smart Guards of Honour for visiting personages when necessary. A drum and bugle band was begun, and named No 33 Platoon. Instruments were paid for by the MG Company and by Wellworthy. The band lasted for 18 months, before conscription of many members caused it to close down.

MG versus a Tank

G Company was, at one point, asked to carry out a military exercise to show how certain weapons were to be used. Company Sergeant-Major Warwick came up with idea of stopping a tank (borrowed from the MG Works) by laying a 'necklace' of mines across the road (the company used the MG test track for this). The men wired the explosives to a battery and detonators. Four men acted as tank crew. They then made a 'field-gun' out of plywood and cardboard. The 'crew' of this were made of straw and sacks. The plan was to fire the gun at the tank, and, with the tank stopped, others would 'attack' it with small arms and overwhelm the by now anxious crew. It all worked well, and it was felt much was learned.

In one mock attack to blow up MG and Wellworthy, the Home Guard acted as enemy paratroops. One man was disguised in an old mac and wellington boots, and tried to enter MG directly to plant explosives. He was captured, and then the alarm was triggered. This brought about shouts, bangs and flashes. Somehow the attack carried over to Marcham Common, as the factory guard counter-attacked. Finally the exercise was called off, but some Home Guard 'parachutists' were so well hidden the Umpire had to send men out to find them and call them in.

One exercise had to stop prematurely one evening, as a senior NCO had to open his pub. After another such manoeuvre near the edge of town, complaints were received that Home Guard men were going from garden to garden on their exercises, leaping over fences and frightening some of the elderly residents.

There were of course many unsung jobs which were every bit as important as the others. Norah Jones, whose husband Sam went away to war with the RAF, worked at riveting instrument panels on fighter aircraft. Soon after this, the company was advertising for lady drivers, so she applied, and was soon able to drive anything. This included a limousine in which she collected a Minister from Oxford Station. Nancy McCormick spent much time repairing the workforce's overalls.

1941 – MG Lays off Men

Other more fundamental changes were in the type of skills required in the change from civilian to war work. While MG was at the stage between civil motor production and war work, what became clear was that a set of workforce skills different from that of peacetime would be required. Steps were taken to clear factory space for war production, and to remove the now unwanted civilian car parts to a storage place. A disused basement was found in West Saint Helen Street, about 1½ miles across

Riveting work: one of the many intensive skills needed to produce GI aircraft at Abingdon in 1944.

town. However, it was some considerable time before the floor-space and the workforce would find productive war work. This, according to MG manager Cecil Kimber, was the reason for 21 skilled and semi-skilled men being dismissed in 1941.

From the employees' point of view the dismissals were due to management bloody-mindedness, having the aim of getting rid of men who were trying to recruit colleagues to the Amalgamated Engineering Union. The men made the case that since their dismissal, other skilled men had been taken on, so they could not really have been redundant.

After calls for help to the District Secretary of the Amalgamated Engineering Union, the case was then heard by the relevant government official, Mr Robinson, the Industrial Relations Officer for southern England. This led to an appeal by the men to the Industrial Relations Appeal Board. Its decision was that MG did have a surplus of certain workforce skills, but that the company had failed to follow the correct procedure, of consulting the workforce before announcing redundancies. This means that there was a wrongful dismissal, and so the men should be reinstated or compensated.

1942 – Saxton Arms Landlord in Fight

In town, life went on much as normal. Edward William Brooks, landlord of the Saxton Arms in Saxton Road, and ex-Surrey cricketer, was summoned for assaulting Thomas Frederick Knight on 23rd December, 1942. Knight was chairman of the MG Welfare Committee, which was responsible for the distribution of chocolate and cigarettes obtained through the canteen. On that December day he saw Brooks taking out cigarettes and chocolate, and asked him not to do so as the Welfare Committee had this in hand. Brooks remarked that this had done him out of a job. One suspects a loss of 'a nice little earner' too.

Later, Knight saw Brooks again distributing the goods, and asked him not to. Brooks replied that he did not care for the Welfare Committee and punched Knight on the jaw. Knight had to report to the first aid room as a result. Knight denied he had given Brooks provocation.

Knight stated that at the time he did not know Brooks was acting under orders. Knight denied using bad language and that he said; "I don't know why a f------ stranger should come in here and sell cigarettes."

Brooks stated that Mr Andrew, a charge-hand, asked him to give up part of his dinner hour in order to collect the cigarettes and chocolates for distribution. He went to the canteen where there was a rumpus. He put down his stock and went to Mr Andrew, who told him: "I asked you to do a job and you must do it." Together they went to the canteen and collected the goods, afterwards returning to the stores, where Brooks started to sell them. Knight came in and for 3-4 minutes argued with Mr Andrew, and again said he did not know why strangers should come here and sell chocolates and cigarettes.

Christopher Thomas Andrew of 42 Bath Street said he gave Brooks orders to collect the goods because the man detailed for the job could not be spared. Brooks told him that Knight had prevented him from collecting the goods. Andrew stated; "That doesn't come off; I am in charge of the Maintenance Section and I do not like others overriding me."

With Brooks, he collected the goods, and went to the office where he obtained a list of men who were to receive the goods, and he started to sell them. Knight came into the room in an agitated manner and Andrew told him to get out as he had no business there.

In the end Brooks was bound over for £5 to keep the peace for 6 months, and it was decided that the assault was committed under provocation.

1942 – MG Sports and Vegetables Day

In July 1942, the MG Sports Club organised a sports day for the staff. At a time when the Blitz on London was still going on, and Nazi forces were racing across Russia in Operation Barbarossa, Mr N K Willis, the honorary secretary, and his staff, compiled a programme of sports, flower and vegetable competitions, and sideshows.

Examples of the sports events, among many others, are: 100 yards run for youths, won by Mr Clapperton; three-legged race won by T Owen and Mrs Lawrence; throwing the cricket ball, won by Mr Longshaw. In the tug o' war, the MG Upper Deck A Department beat T Department.

In the Fruit and Vegetable Show, the Collection of Vegetables event was won by W H Gerring, Best Green Cabbage won by I A Watts … and so on. Other names which appear several times in these events were H A Argyle, A B Carter, and E R Edwards.

Best Fruit Cake was baked by I F Lawrence, and Best Knitwear Suitable for Adults was created by Miss M Cox.

Then it was back to construction of engines for Lancaster bombers, cockpits for Albemarle aircraft, and the building of several types of armoured vehicle.

1942 – MG Factory Fire-Watching Offences

Nine employees were fined varying amounts for failing to attend fire-watching duties on various dates in February 1942. The reason given by most was that they just did not believe the town would be bombed, and generally were proved correct in this. It was also why most people did not bother going into air raid shelters when German aircraft flew over; local people knew these were bound for Birmingham and Coventry, or were returning from there.

Pleas of Not Guilty were entered by four, while the others pleaded Guilty.

On 3rd April, 1940, five MG workers were fined £5 each for non-attendance. The fine was deliberately heavy to discourage others from the same behaviour, and to emphasise that absence from duty, either at work, ARP duty or any other national service, was a criminal offence.

1944 – Fire at the MG Store in West Saint Helen Street

At the beginning of the Second World War in 1939, the factory had to prepare for war work, and this meant removing civilian car production for the duration; at that time no one could know how long that would be. The site chosen was a disused basement in the Clarke's clothing factory at the bottom of West Saint Helen Street, close to the church. It was also used as a machine shop for small tank parts.

In 1944 the factory caught fire, and a story slowly developed about what happened next. Iris Dixon's (née Taphouse) father, Eddie, was on duty that night. One version of the story, which many still believe, is that the fire caused so much damage (in part because the store's wooden floor collapsed on to the car parts stored in the basement) that the only solution was to concrete the whole lot over and forget them. Perhaps, in a thousand years, archaeologists would dig down and wonder why these possibly sacred motor parts were buried, perhaps in some form of ritual worship of the internal combustion engine.

A rather more realistic story is that indeed many of the parts stored there were damaged. However such was the urgent need for precious components and metals that as many parts as possible were salvaged and recycled. Only then was the basement covered over permanently. Peter Neal believes this is the true story of the 1944 fire.

Roy 'Titch' Belcher recalls, as a child, watching the fire: he was on his way home from school at the time.

1945 – MG Workers see 'Tempest' Fly-past

To counter the onslaught from V1 flying bombs, the government developed an aircraft – the Tempest – which was designed to fly and meet the bombs, and either shoot them down or tip their wings with the Tempest's wing, and cause them to dive in to the ground, or preferably the sea.

The MG factory took on the job of manufacturing the forward and trailing edges of the wings and spars on behalf of the Ministry of Aircraft Production. The Minister was very impressed, and arranged for a squadron of nine Spitfires and a Tempest II to give a flying demonstration over the factory by way of an appreciation of the Works' efforts. The whole workforce turned out to watch this, and to share lunch with the pilots afterwards, some of whom were Battle of Britain veterans. Mr H Ryder gave a speech.

Tempest MkII flyover observed by MG staff.

Iris Dixon

Iris began at MG in 1942, having previously worked at Wellworthy Pistons close by. Her family came from the Isle of Dogs, East London, in 1941, but had moved due to the bombing. What she and many other girls really wanted to do was to join the Women's Royal Naval Service (WRNS) but her father refused permission. She recalls seeing V1 flying bombs and other aircraft over London – her school was bombed and many killed. Just outside the bottom of their garden was a barrage balloon site, and the RAF crew lived close by in tents.

At MG her job was in Tempest Aircraft Inspection, using a Vernier, which is a small graduated scale for obtaining fractional subdivisions on a fixed main scale, in this case to measure the thickness of the Tempests' wing struts.

Iris' day at MG began at 7.30am and ended at 6pm. The women's hair had to be put up out of the way, which accounted for some of the fashions of the time, both in hair and in work clothes.

She was issued with a Works card which had to be shown when entering the factory. Her clock number was 25527/1107. She thought the discipline there rather strict, "but then it had to be." The general view, though, is that discipline was 'laid back,' provided everyone pulled their weight. But as Sue Stevens once found, there was something chilling about receiving an instruction to report to the Personnel Office – you knew you were in for it. Sue had to face this finger wagging for having spent too much time talking to her family members when collecting the post.

Iris recalls that a common problem amongst the staff was dermatitis, which appears to have come from metal slurry, and treatment could be obtained at the MG medical centre. There, it seems, the nurses always presumed that girls reporting sick were in fact pregnant. Of course, some were.

Pay day was on a Friday with cash in a packet – women always worked at a rate lower than that of the men, but this was also true nationally. A man would come around with a big box – you gave him your relevant clock number, and he gave you your wage packet.

Once off shift, many of the staff were required to attend civil defence and Home Guard duties. Iris' duties were in the Abbey area where the headquarters building once was. Iris does not recall being much bothered with air raid sirens, one of which was placed at the top of the stair tower in the County Hall and manned by Home Guards.

Iris had five sisters, two of whom worked on the Albemarle bomber aircraft, at what was called 'top aircraft,' ie, at the top of the aircraft being constructed. Albemarles, nicknamed 'Marbles,' were being partly constructed at MG, with other parts of the assembly elsewhere. Their line foreman there was George Plumber. One of Iris' elder sisters was a secretary, which is what Iris really wanted to be.

White Feathers

Iris' Dad was a security man at MG, and when he began there he was given a white feather signifying cowardice. It may have signified local ill-feeling towards Londoners, calling them 'Berkshire Cockneys' or 'Dirty Cockneys.' The fact was that he had been in the Royal Artillery at The Somme in 1916, and suffered from shell-shock. Iris states that many Londoners were resented in Abingdon, but gradually the town came to accept them. Some live in Abingdon even now.

Music and Dance

During the morning, beginning at 10am, the tannoy at the factory would broadcast the BBC's Light Programme of popular tunes: *Music While You Work*, and they would all sing along with it, dressed in their dungarees or boiler suits.

Iris had heard of the job at MG from a friend in her previous employment. He was a gentleman who could dance well, and had his own band. He was some years older than her, but asked her to marry him. Her Dad – again – refused permission as he felt she was too young. Her friend did, however, give her a crossbar-ride home occasionally.

Iris Entertains

Iris was a good singer and toured local US, RAF and army camps with a band. One band she sung with was 'The Racketeers' who regularly played at the MG Club when it was in West Saint Helen Street. They often played in the Corn Exchange too. She sang such tunes of the time as *Old Rocking Chair, Let Us Be Sweethearts, A Sin to Tell a Lie, Mexicali Rose, Have You Ever Been Lonely* and *We'll Meet Again*.

The club upstairs in the Clarke's building in West Saint Helen Street was known as the 'Honky Tonk,' especially at the time the American servicemen were in town, and this was where, later, Jimmy Cox met his future wife Pat. The club was not immune from crime, because on one occasion a burglar gained entry and stayed there while the club was locked for the night. Somehow the police were alerted and came in, but could see no sign of breaking and entering. They looked around and finally found the thief under the snooker table.

At the club, young RAF aircrew would arrive and sit there in full flying kit. She has not yet understood how they were supposed to get back to the airfield if an alarm went off. Would they all be collected by the RAF people?

Eddie at the Organ

Finally Iris married Eddie Dixon, with an American sergeant as their best man – who became a monk after returning to the USA. Eddie was the pianist and organist at the social club. At one time he had accompanied silent films in the Stert Street Pavilion cinema, a role earlier filled by Mrs Edie Perrior, who was "tall and rather flamboyant with bad teeth – but very nice." Eddie was a skilled mechanic, and a member of the Home Guard. He

Eddie Dixon at the piano.

worked at testing MG's tanks on Gore Hill, south of Abingdon. Eddie was also, incidentally, a noted billiard player at the MG Social Club.

MG also boasted a Dramatic Society, known as IADOME – 'It All Depends on Me.'

When not singing with the band, Iris and friends might go to the Regal Cinema. The nearest air raid shelter was in the basement of J N Paul's shoe shop at 26, High Street, and was constructed by the Cowley Tiling and Concrete Company of Radley Road. Mr Paul was nicknamed 'Mr Spittle,' and would often let customers buy shoes on the instalment plan.

Iris left MG when pregnant with her son Barry, but was told she still had to work somewhere. She found employment at the old Stert Street cinema, by then converted, and made mess tins for the army.

The End of the War

Like many other companies, MG had its VE Day parties, as did the residents of Gainsborough Green where Iris lived. Pictures of these town events can be found in the *North Berks Herald* of the time.

MG took on many Polish staff at the end of the war, and also some German ex-prisoners-of-war, to whom two of Iris' friends got married. Other MG girls became GI (US servicemen) brides and moved to the United States.

Iris and Eddie's sons Barry and Clive both worked at MG, and Clive – known to all as 'Cozy' – eventually left there to work as a drummer with

29

Frank Ifield, who had hits with *I Remember You* and *She Taught me to Yodel*. Clive also has a band called 'Barbary Coast.'

Tanks for the Memories

As a child Roy Belcher remembers watching armoured vehicles being driven from the factory along Cemetery Road, left into Spring Road and up to the junction with Faringdon Road, then turning towards town and the station. As the tanks turned towards town, they would often scrape against the kerbstones and damage them. To repair them it seems the Town Council simply turned them upside down. Roy believes some of those kerbstones are still there.

Roy well recalls in earlier years, watching World War Two tanks being driven to the Abingdon GWR station and presumably loaded up for transportation to the south coast.

An MG driver for these tanks, which were also submerged in a factory water facility to check for leaks, was Olly Pearce.

Interestingly, during World War Two, the whole of the southern bypass around Oxford was one vast tank park. It was also where the city buses were parked to avoid having them all destroyed by one air raid on their Oxford garage.

Chapter 3

Life at the Factory

Postwar Ill-feeling

Clearly, many men at MG during the war period were exempt from military service, having reserved occupations. However, a considerable number of men and women did enter the armed services, and it was some of these who felt a sense of resentment on their return.

The reason for their resentment was that they had gone off to war and risked their lives, while those who stayed behind were earning good money with all their extra work, gaining experience and qualifications – and promotions. As a result, when the servicemen and women returned, they felt they had been treated very badly both by the company and by the government. The person who related this has asked to remain anonymous, but was a regular in the 'Ox' pub in Oxford Road in the late 1980s.

1946 – Arthur Way's Appeal

In 1946, Henry Arthur Way, resident of John Morris Road, Abingdon, returned from the war having served in the Royal Artillery since 1939. He had worked at MG before the war, and was hoping for reinstatement in his old job on the chassis line, where he had previously worked for six years.

On his return he was told there was no vacancy for him in his old job, but was offered, and he accepted, a job on the finishing line. This went on for 26 weeks, after which he was taken off that job, and put on tanks, which were still being manufactured at that time.

He was then moved on to the chassis line on piecework rates, but according to him was not allowed to complete a job because of 'outside interference' by members of management. He complained about this, and finally gave notice to end his employment, applying again for reinstatement in his original job, on proper terms and conditions, and not on piecework.

Mr Way said the piecework terms on which he went back differed considerably from those in operation before he left for the armed services. He accepted that the terms had been agreed between the management and him, but added that if a man was timed in his work, he should at least be allowed to do it without external interference.

He lost his appeal at the Oxford Reinstatement Committee, which stated that as the law now was, Mr Way had no case.

Elsie's Turban

In 1948 MG took on its first female operative in the Rectification Department, her name was Elsie Cumming. Elsie, known as 'Jock' because of her Scottish origins, always wore a red and white turban, and a painting of her can be found in the Abingdon underpass, where she is depicted in her turban and black overalls, standing under the letters 'MG'. Each time her family walks past they shout "Hello, Gran!"

Elsie was on duty one day in 1956, when she saw an elderly gentleman in an old mac walking through her department. She shouted: "Hey, you're not allowed in here!"

The gentleman turned out to be William Morris, Lord Nuffield himself.

Elsie Cumming.

Bob Matthews – Where's MG Gone?

In the prewar period, a bus came from Oxford each day and delivered workers to the entrance at Cemetery Road. According to Dutchy Holland, they seemed to get off the bus in the same order every day: John Bull, Fred Hemmings, Reg Brindley, Mr Fisher and Billy Wilkins and others.

First though, one had to know about the bus service, or cycle or walk to the factory. Bob Matthews' Dad was an employee in the early days of MG. He turned up for work on his first day, and just could not find the factory. It seems that the Ock Street Fair was blocking his way, and he did at last find his way there. He was a mechanic, and recalls seeing MG-produced tanks on their way to trials near Gore Hill on what is now the A34.

Matthews senior worked in MG from 1929 to 1963. He was the race mechanic for the great Italian driver Tazio Nuvolari, and often drove him to Brooklands circuit and back. Alec Hounslow, while still an apprentice at Morris Garages, served as riding mechanic to Nuvolari when they won the 1933 Ulster TT in an MG Magnette.

Matthews senior was a good tool inventor and, seeing a need for a particular tool or an improvement to one, went to work to produce it. He once created a device called the 'little black boy.' This was a pump attached to the vehicle's steering column when air had got into the hydraulic fluid. The pump fitted there and onto the floor, and bled the brakes and clutch of air simultaneously by compressed air. Apparently, it saved many man-hours doing it all by hand.

Incidentally, Bob's uncle was once the driver of the Abingdon 'Bunk' engine, which ran between Radley and Abingdon.

Bob's Dad died in the medical centre at MG, having suffered a cerebral haemorrhage. Only then did Bob get a job at the Works, as his Dad did not believe in nepotism. Bob began on assembly of MGB carburettors, then worked on the body of Sprites and Midgets, and finally the trim line making fascia panels.

Family Atmosphere

Something which all MG ex-employees comment upon is the 'family atmosphere' which prevailed there, and the fact that just about everyone thoroughly enjoyed their work. There was also a great spirit of mutual support between them as the following stories show.

Derek Powell remembers such names as the Purbricks (Carol and Arthur), Drew (Derek married one, Pat, who had been the Beauty Queen

The jovial atmosphere of a happy work family, exemplified at the MG Social Club.

34

one year), Stimpson (father and 3 sons Bernard, Brian and Alan), the Morgans and many others.

If a small DIY job was needed to be done at home, MG staff always produced someone who was able to do it, be it electric work, carpentry, plumbing, bricklaying or whatever. Many men who were later made redundant set up in self-employment with their redundancy money, for example Andy Glass with Palmer Plumbing. Fred Stevens notes that Dave Neil and Arthur Purbrick were very quick and efficient with window-glazing and carpentry, having done some work on Fred's house.

Sue Stevens

It seems that romance was never too far away in the Works. Sue and Fred Stevens met through the MG football club (married in 1972). Sue's first job when she left school at 15 was at the car factory. She worked at MG from 1963 to 1967, along with Dad and five uncles. Miss Brewer the Personnel Officer interviewed her, but it was more like an introduction. They took her on as a tea-girl, wearing dark blue overalls, and she worked in the 'Service' department. Another pairing was that of Frank Beams who met his wife at MG.

The Service department was under the Service Manager, and ran from the 1930s until 1963. Customers would bring in their MGs to this large department for service or repair. The department also incorporated Service Stores, which received and despatched orders from all over the country, including garages and private individuals.

Sue worked eight hours a day, and felt it was a good place to work. Her workplace was next to the Austin Healey line, and her job was to collect the post, and similar jobs, which allowed her to wander round the factory talking to uncles, friends and so on. More than once she was told not to waste time. Then Sue was promoted to the factory's own Driving School and was taught to drive. People came from all over UK to learn and to take a test.

Some employees learned there, but other people from outside MG (possibly BMC?) came to learn to drive heavy vehicles or cars, and to take advanced driving courses etc. The school secretary was Olive Mercer, and in charge was Chief Driving Instructor, Harry Shillabeer, who had been a police constable, and trained at Hendon as a member of the Metropolitan Police Force. One instructor, Harry Bradford, later set up a school on his own in town. Heather Grant was once taken by the school to Silverstone to ride as a passenger on the skidpan.

Then BL paid for Sue to go to college where she learned office skills and typing, and its endless practice of A-S-D-F-;-L-K-J and so on. She worked with many ex-schoolfriends, and attended the Social Club in West Saint Helen Street with Mum and Dad. Her dad was Ivor Morgan from Neath, who had been posted to Abingdon when in the RAF, while her mum was an Abingdonian.

Sue bought a new car with a special deal (£500?) but it had been fitted with a secondhand radiator which 'exploded' outside St Aldate's police station. The police helped fix it, and Sue wrote to Lord Don Stokes about the radiator but, it seems, received only an unsatisfactory reply.

Elsewhere at the Factory …

One lady who wishes to remain anonymous relates that at one point she was secretary to an MG manager. She had been transferred from another part of the factory and did not really want this position. Miss […] had joined as a tea-girl in 1963 at 15 years of age, having responded to the headmistress' call for girls to be interviewed for MG. She attended an interview at the Personnel Office and won a position, and was soon spending a day at college, paid for by MG, learning typing and office skills. She was sent to work as a typist at the Riley Car Club in the main building upstairs. Then it was back to Material Controls, which soon amalgamated with Production to become Production and Materials. It was then she was moved to the manager's secretary job.

While walking through the assembly area one day, dressed in her smart green Crimplene suit, she suddenly slipped and fell, right in front of the assembly workers, who saw what had happened and let out a very loud cheer.

It seems that she and her husband had been trying for a baby for some time with no luck, unfortunately. Mrs […] as she now was, had met her husband in 1964, and they married in 1968. It seems that the three previous secretaries in what was now her job had left because they had become pregnant. Having accepted the position, she was a little surprised some months after having taken up the job in the manager's office in 1973, to find she too had (at last) become pregnant. Was it something in the office?

Football is the Game

Fred Stevens, on leaving school, began work at Coxeter's furniture removal firm at about £4 a week in 1964. Fred played goalkeeper for Abingdon Town FC in the 1960s. He just missed National Service, but would quite like to have done it. He also played football for MG 'to make numbers up,' although he didn't work there at first. In fact, he seems to have been talent-spotted by Norman Higgins, Chief Accountant at MG. He saw Fred's playing and offered him a job at MG, which Fred took gratefully as it meant a considerable payrise. Fred's first foreman was Jimmy 'Simm' Simpson in Goods Inwards, where he eventually earned £40 a week. Jimmy Simpson had served in the Royal Pioneer Corps in the war, mainly loading and unloading railway trucks, digging trenches and filling sandbags. He had been working in Goods Inwards a long time, and knew the contents of every bin in the stores. However small a screw, he could go straight to it, and there were 'hundreds' of bins in Goods Inwards.

Men from the MG Inspections Department, sporting their grey coats.

Obtaining the job was possibly helped by the fact that Fred's uncles Dick and Ken worked there. Three other football team members obtained work at MG at that time: Andy Glass, Hayden Matthews and Peter Weston. When first shown around the MG factory, the line staff all sang "Blue is the Colour, Football is the Game," as they knew how Fred and some others had got their jobs – again, no interview as such, but were spoken to by Miss Payne (from Drayton) and told "You are to work in Goods Inwards." In the canteen, they had to tolerate lots of jibes about 'footballers getting jobs.'

Fred unloaded goods on wooden pallets from lorries before taking them to the Inspection Department. Here were many inspectors and they wore grey coats (foremen wore white) and would inspect about 1 in 10 of each delivered item unless told to inspect each one: looms, headlights, sidelights, windscreens (which had been imported), etc.

"Up the Line!"

Fred put his name down for the line as pay was better. He was put on the Trim Deck. The bodies came down from Pressed Steel Oxford, ready-painted and stamped with an ID number. He was positioned half way down the MGB Line. Fred recalls that you didn't have to work too fast once you had mastered the job. He was taught by Dave Carter, a Line Relief man. When jobs there were done, the cry went up: "Up The Line," and the car was pushed to the next station.

At first he was on piece-work, which ended in the 1960s with the advent of Time and Motion, then on Measured Day work, which meant that if you finished your quota of cars, about 42 of them, you could go home. Sometimes they played cards, which was often Crib. Then he was on line relief from the early 1970s. This meant he could be required to do any job on the line. Fred hated working with windscreens as he saw this as a mucky, greasy job, and hated having to be relief on it.

Then Fred was on toilet relief; each man had a few minutes per day for toilet visits (often used as cigarette breaks) and Fred would do their job while they were away.

Another way of having a few minutes off, legally, was to go to the Works barber shop in 'A' block between the press shop and the assembly area. Haircuts would cost about 1/6d.

Wages were paid in brown wage packets, which was quite normal nationally. Fred Stevens once lost his wages – he'd placed the packet in his back pocket and parked in what is now the MG Memorial Park on Ock Street. He went to take it out of his pocket, but it had gone. Word got round the factory, and on the Monday and Tuesday a collection was made and Fred was presented with an envelope which actually contained more than his wages had been. Fred was moved by this gesture, and sees it still as the kind of camaraderie that was typical of the people at MG Abingdon.

Mervyn Chadwick worked for a while at MG, on the Midget line which was next to the MGB line. He was in the Salvation Army, and very good on cornet and bugle. While a relief man did Mervyn's job, he would play Christmas carols in which everyone joined in. Indeed there was always much singing on the line, especially on a Friday.

A quite normal event was for each party of the Works, say each

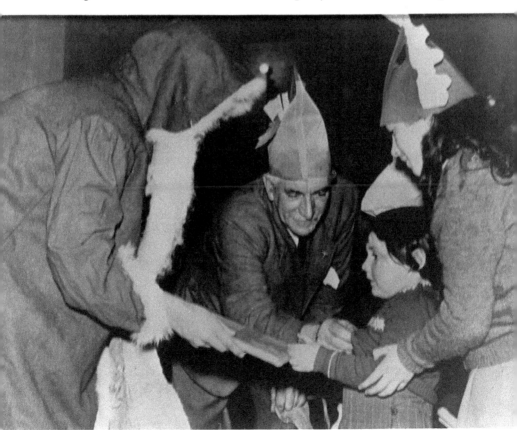

Gift giving and a Father Christmas (Mr C Martin) at the 1954 MG Christmas party.

production line, and other departments, to have a party in town, for example at Christmas, just for their own members. Sue and Fred once had a 'line do' in Hanney Village Hall. Barry Dodd organised it – a dinner and dance. These two had heard that quite recently Sue and Fred had read the gas and electric meters the wrong way round, so their bills came back very high indeed. Arthur Hedges and Barry Dodd heard about this and built huge electric meters to present to them at the dance.

There was also a huge autograph book passed round for all to sign, as Fred had been asked some time earlier by a young football fan for an autograph.

... And Almost a Lost Job

Glyn Walters tells a story about leaks in the roof of 'A' block. The structure was such that there was guttering between the 'A' shaped gables – as can be seen now in the units on the left of Colwell Road, which were once 'B' block. The downpipes were placed at regular spaces along the guttering, but were unreliable, so Glyn was required to come up with a scheme for improvement. What happened was that the exterior of the roof was covered in plastic and the downpipes plugged. The Works Fire Brigade under Cyril Cox was then instructed to pump water onto the roof to check for leakages. It all held and then Glyn decided to remove the downpipe plugs for a further check, which is when gallons of water plunged down on to the workshop below and caused everything to be stopped. Glyn felt he had been lucky to have kept his job after that.

Another tale Glyn tells is that in the Board Room the clock, which was of a hexagonal shape, contained no number 2. He says that this was because lunch for them was always from 1pm until just after 2pm, so with an 'occasional extension,' the number 2 was irrelevant. That clock, it seems, is now in Derek Powell's house.

He notes too, perhaps with an enigmatic smile, that the Dog House pub at Frilford was always considered to be an annex to the Board Room, as sometimes quite important decisions had to be made there, especially with important visitors.

He once received instructions to build a special room – he was given the dimensions, and was told it had to have a four foot wide door, while there had to be special security measures such as keypads. Some equipment was delivered, and everyone was itching to find out what all the high security was about.

The great secret was in fact a high security Telex line, the first facsimile machine, and all this was linked with Honda, and its development of new vehicles. Extra security was needed, so a Director's signature had to be obtained before one could use the photocopier. Before this it was all Gestetner spirit duplicators.

Irene Grant (née Bennett)

Irene's dad worked all over the factory from its beginning in Abingdon in 1929. Initially he was given a six-month trial. Three of her dad's brothers worked there too, as did one of their wives, in Personnel. One brother stayed at the factory until 1980, except for a break for his National Service. Irene was there from 1948 to the 1950s, working on the MGTC models (all women) and MGTD model line, next to the Riley line, on the Trim Deck. She was, like her dad, a keen angler and belonged to the 'Anchor' angling club.

She and her friends enjoyed dances, which they could go to three times a week: Monday, Wednesday and Friday at the Corn Exchange. Sometimes they would travel by bus to Oxford for dances and films.

Irene met her husband (a Scot) at a dance in Abingdon's Church Hall behind Saint Nicolas' Church. He was a fireman at the RAF camp. Then they could go to the MG club for good bands, but had to queue if it was

The MG Switchboard in action.

41

MG cars on the production line at Abingdon.

43

a really good one. The club in West Saint Helen Street was known as the 'Honky Tonk,' and during the war (and just after it) there were many US servicemen there. It was quite normal in those days for whole families to go there together for the evening.

Heather, her daughter, left school at 15, beginning at MG as a tea-girl, earning £4.19.6d a week. She hated the 'ugly' blue overalls. Later she worked on the company switchboard, greeting callers to Abingdon 0235-251, later 25251, with "Good Morning, MG Car Company," or possibly "Leyland Assembly Plant Abingdon," or later "Good morning, BL MG Car Division" – a real mouthful.

Heather recalls that there was an annual Miss MG beauty contest, held in the Caldecott Road Social Club. One girl won it several times. There was a tote run there too, with good cash prizes.

She describes, too, how she worked in an office facing Marcham Road, and the only escape in case of fire was to sit themselves in a pulley and leather harness arrangement and 'walk it' down the outside wall to the ground.

Daily Routine

The working day started at 7.30am, and you were allowed three minutes leeway. After that you lost a quarter-of-an-hour's pay. If you worked on the line, and someone was late, there were people known as 'sick-reliefs' or 'spare man,' so that production was not affected. An example of such a need was when factory firemen were called out. Such relief men were high-fliers, because they could do any of the jobs required on the assembly line. There was an hour for lunch for which you clocked in and out, 12.30 to 1.30pm.

There was a mid-morning break, and most workers had tea and coffee delivered by the tea-boys. One problem here was that some people had bigger cups than others, but they all wanted them filled right up.

In the morning the tannoy played *Music While You Work* from the BBC Light Programme, introduced by the tune *Calling All Workers* composed by Eric Coates, famous for composing the theme to the film *The Dam Busters*. The programme featured bands of many different sorts playing light music and popular tunes. The programme had begun in June 1940 and ended in September 1967. In its later years it became popular with people at home, and with motorists.

Each person had a number of tasks to do to the car as it arrived at their workstation. For example, fit headlamps and connect them to the wiring loom (which someone else had fitted) and then fit the radiator grille. All the jobs would have been set by time-and-motion people, and would have to be completed in a set time. The car was then hand-pushed to the next place, and the new one arrived. The production requirement for the day was posted at the end of the line so that all could see it. Even when the correct number was completed, not everyone went home then, but stayed around until 4.30 when the hooter went.

On these occasions the unions made sure that this process was a 'good earner', and overplayed the time needed for each car to be constructed.

Vito Orlando

Vito Orlando worked at MG from 1957 to 1980 – 23 years. He attended school at Boxhill, and fondly recalls watching the MG cars being driven through town from the factory to the railway station to be loaded on to trains for transport to Southampton, and then to the USA. As a result he told himself, "I want to work at MG." He left school at 14 because of the way his birthday fell (April) and started there as 'Shop boy', or tea-boy, beginning with work on Austin-Healey Sprites, helping the line operators, and would often be required to make up small assemblies such as wiper-motors or put brackets on. As tea-boy he was moved regularly between departments while he was between 15 and 18 years old, and he received no full pay until the age of 21. Incidentally, the women only got about 5/8ths of a man's pay.

At 21, he was in the Development Department on such work as grinding valves, then became a relief man and then assembly production foreman.

Later, he worked on the Morris Traveller, making 20 per day. One of his jobs was placing 'headlining' (inside roof covering), which required him to hold tacks in his mouth and hammer them into the vehicle with a magnetic hammer. He had to complete three an hour. The line was only as fast as the slowest man and, on piece-work, the slowest man was of course very unpopular.

Keeping Trim

Vito spent some time on the trim deck fitting fascia panels, steering rack, carpets, wire looms, headlamps. The car was then lowered down to the track and received clutch and gearbox, batteries and seats. Then it was sent to the end of the line.

He recalls, in the days before monocoque construction came in (where the body and chassis were in one piece), going into the press and welding shop, without any protective kit, and describes the many blue welding flashes and men in masks. That all changed when the combined body and chassis came in, and far less making of parts was necessary. Another recollection was of the early days, when metal parts needed to be degreased. The smell was very strong – a bit like pear-drops – and breathing it became known as a great cure for coughs and colds.

Paul Radcliffe Binnington – 'Tim'

Paul Binnington, always known as Tim, ran a department at MG known as the 'Show Shop,' which prepared vehicles for motor shows such as Earls Court, and created cutaway parts to show the detail of engines and other parts of cars.

One customer had owned a black MG TF, but had smashed it up and it needed some serious repairs. Finally he decided to give it to John Thornley, the Managing Director, who put it into the Show Shop where it was rebuilt and put on show.

In 1957 a new MG was being turned out every 45 minutes, 85% of these for export. During that year, Tim's family was struck by tragedy. At 10.42am on 5th March 1957, an RAF Beverley four-engined transport aircraft, number XH 117, took off from RAF Abingdon, bound for Akrotiri in Cyprus. It carried 17 passengers and 5 crew, plus a number

Engine cutaways and models are an informative feature of MG exhibitions, such as this model of a 4-cylinder displayed at Abingdon Museum in the late 1990s.

of RAF guard-dogs. It weighed 70 tons and had a wingspan of 162 feet; an enormous aircraft. As it climbed to around 500 feet, an engine failed. The pilot turned the aircraft back towards the airfield and another engine failed. Attempting to land in a field the aircraft struck power cables and then a group of elm trees. The port wing was torn from the body of the aircraft which then swung round and, at 11.03am, 18 minutes after take-off, smashed into the ground in the village of Sutton Wick, 2 miles south of Abingdon, directly on top of a brick-built house and a pre-fabricated one, somersaulted and exploded.

In the prefab house was 50-year-old Mrs Muriel Katherine Gaburn Binnington, Tim's wife. She would have been killed instantly and could have known nothing about it, having sustained a fractured skull and cerebral damage. Fortunately, at the time of the crash, their three eldest children were at work, and the youngest was at school.

Locally a fund was set up for the victims, which raised around £100. They also received Air Ministry compensation, although it took about three years to come through, and until then the local authority rehoused Tim's family in a council house in Kennington.

On the night of the crash, the family was accommodated by relatives living nearby. Mrs Binnington's funeral was at Headington Crematorium. There is today an oaken memorial to the victims, standing in the village of Sutton Wick. Incidentally, the Binnington's son, Antony, later took up motor-racing, driving MGs in competition.

Steve Palmer

He was one of the few 'outsiders' working on contract at the MG factory in 1967, the time when the Austin-Healey 'badged' MGC was being developed. This project may have eventually failed because its performance was heavily criticised by the press, in particular the fact that it was 'nose-heavy', but also there was a good deal of competition from the Triumph TR6 at the same time. Steve says he was one of the few non-MG people who actually saw the car during its early development.

It happened like this: Steve, at the time (1967), was an apprentice at his family's firm, Palmer's the plumbers. The firm was working to install an overhead gas supply at the Abingdon MG Works on behalf of Southern Gas.

Their supervisor, Tony Bell, drove Steve there to help with the work. Knowing of Steve's interest in cars generally, Tony mentioned that there were some MGBs there with bulges in the bonnets. These were parked in a group around the back, near where the installation work was being carried out. The cars were soon to be announced as the new MGC.

They pulled up behind a silver GT. It was badged not as an MGC but, as Steve recalls it, an Austin-Healey 3000. This was the Austin-Healey version of the MGC range that was cancelled at a late stage of development. It appears that Donald Healey declined to lend his name to it due to its handling characteristics. It had a heavy six-cylinder engine and suffered from oversteer.

Steve recalls an MG worker offering the plumbers 'cheap car cigarette lighters' on a number of occasions.

Double Take

In the 1970s, American TV audiences could see an advertisement for MG cars. It showed a Roadster being transported by aircraft over a desert landscape. An MGB flew out of the back of the aircraft on a carrying assembly, finally a parachute opened and it all floated safely down to earth. Then a young man climbed into the car and calmly drove off.

The reality, according to Steve, was that on the first take, the cameras rolled but the parachute failed to open, and it all hit the desert floor at speed, reducing the dimensions of the car somewhat. Then came the cry: "Second car please!" … and "Take!"

The video advertisement – minus the first take – was, at time of writing, on display in the gallery at Abingdon County Hall Museum, next to one of the last MGBs to be made in Abingdon, sprayed in the gold Jubilee colours by Ernest Herring.

Engineer Killed in Road Accident

In February 1966, a factory planning engineer at MG in Abingdon, Mr David Ashley Giles, single and 35, was killed when his MG 1100 struck a tree at Nuneham Courtenay. His body was released from the wreckage only when the Oxfordshire Fire Brigade cut him free.

Known to his friends as Doug, Mr Giles lived at 2, East Saint Helen Street, Abingdon, sharing a 2nd floor flat with Keith Faulkner. Doug had served an apprenticeship at Morris Motors in Oxford, and was there for seven years, joining MG Abingdon in 1955. He was responsible for all new building work at the Abingdon site.

At that time they could find a very useful car park in the Market Place, the statue of Queen Victoria having been removed in 1946 for that very purpose. An additional benefit, according to Keith, was that the 1st floor was occupied by a dentist, and if one of them had a hangover, they could always ask the dentist for a whiff of oxygen. It was apparently Doug's MG department that designed the MG Social Club in Caldecott Road, but, ironically, he found himself banned from it at one point.

They used the Mousehole Café below the County Hall, and Delamonte's in East Saint Helen Street. The manageress there had a son called George Bartle, who was also an MG apprentice, and later moved to Esso Research.

Taxi!

Accidents can happen anywhere, but fortunately most were less serious than the above. One day, on the line, Mickey Haynes suffered some damage to an eye. The company paid for him to go by taxi to the Eye Hospital in Oxford. He was treated there, but only had enough cash to get part of the way back. He managed as far as Kennington, and had to then make his own way. He managed to hitch a ride and so returned to town.

Tony Barrett

Tony began work one Monday morning in May 1968, and remembers being laid off almost straight away. A check in the local press reveals, however, that the problem was production at MG being disrupted by a strike at Pressed Steel Fisher in Oxford. All car assembly stopped at MG on Monday 29th of May 1968, but began to pick up again on the Tuesday. The Cowley factory, which produced the GT version of the bodies of cars assembled at Abingdon, was on strike for a week. Abingdon was the only British Motor Corporation factory to lay off workers because of the strike. A total of 350 Abingdon workers were affected.

Dick's Wig

Tony Barrett tells a story concerning Dick Seddon. Dick usually wore a wig, and on one occasion he was using a big grease gun which wouldn't operate. He continually squeezed the trigger with no luck, but the pressure

The Marcham Road entrance to the MG factory.

was building inside. Suddenly a squirt of thick black grease shot out of the back of the gun and struck him in the face, knocking his wig off, to the enjoyment of all those nearby.

Philip Bolton

Philip Bolton began at MG in 1963, and stayed until 1979. Before that he had worked on the land around Gozzard's Ford. He spent those 16 years in Goods Inwards with foreman Jimmy Simpson, who was a leading member of the Works Fire Brigade. Philip was often asked to go back on the land, but said that the money at MG was too good in comparison.

There were seven men in Goods Inwards, and Philip thoroughly enjoyed it. The work was better than the line because it was more varied – you were not just an extension of a machine. He would check the quantity of goods coming in, but Goods Inward Inspection, in their grey coats, would check the quality. Work would normally start at 7.30am, but Goods Inward preferred to begin at 7am, and deal with any materials delivered overnight. They had to clock on and off, and each employee had a Works number. There were no women in Goods Inwards, as they tended to

50

work in the office. One section (KD, or 'knocked down') dealt with goods ordered from outside by garages and other customers. The foreman there was Jimmy Roberts who would ask if you wanted overtime, which often came in very handy.

One advantage of his position was that Goods Inwards did not have the usual factory fortnight Works holiday, but used this time instead for stock-taking. They could then take their holidays when they wished.

Interestingly, January 1st was not a holiday as it is now. Although attendance could, according to Keith Faulkner be described as 'slow,' informal agreements were reached where extra cars were produced in the week. This informal arrangement generally meant that New Year's Day could be taken off with no loss of production.

Sign Here!

Tim Davies has the following recollection concerning Goods Inwards. He comments that, in contrast with most British Leyland plants in the 1970s, Abingdon was considered particularly moderate. Whilst the news cameras seemed at times to be permanently camped outside the gates in Cowley Road and union leader 'Red Robbo' was causing merry mayhem at Longbridge, MG just appeared to trundle on year after year with very few issues.

However, something had obviously irked the lads in Goods Inwards one particular day, as they refused to sign-off what would normally be a regular delivery. There had been an instruction not to accept anything that couldn't be checked against official engineering specifications, and they received an urgent phone call to the office to supply a technical drawing of … brake-fluid.

Obviously a job for the apprentice. Quickly, grab a fresh drawing sheet, allocate a drawing number from the register, fill in title block, copy out specification (Tim did suggest drawing a splash of fluid in the middle of the sheet, but was advised against it), get check print, gain engineering and management sign-off, run off issued blueprint, sprint down to Goods Inwards at Gate 4 and present it to the Quality Inspector.

He very slowly and ceremoniously laid the print out on a desk to study, then sauntered over to the stack of barrels and diligently compared the details on the drawing to the labels on the delivery. Without a word he turned to his colleague and nodded. The note was duly signed and the delivery driver was, gratefully, free to go.

A well-known site: the former MG offices next to Kimber House – now home of the MG Car Club.

Peter Jeffries

Pete attended Bury Street School and later Saint Nicolas School in Boxhill Road. When he left in 1955, his first job was at Pavlova. He trained there as an electrician, and the company gave him time to attend day classes at the technical school in Conduit Road, and evening classes at Brooks Polytechnic. He completed his Ordinary and Higher National Certificates to become qualified.

He remarks that Pavlova was a difficult place to work in, with the smell of the piles of pelts and the various chemicals making for a fairly unpleasant environment. But work in Abingdon at that time, at least work with any prospects, was at Pavlova, MG or Morland's Brewery.

While working as an electrician at Pavlova there was a certain amount of overlap with the MG Works, as the two plants occasionally swapped tradesmen who, as a result, had unrestricted access to both works. In this way Pete became a familiar figure in both places.

He notes that pay at Pavlova was lower than MG, where in 1955 he could earn £29 per week, but at Pavlova only £17 per week.

No Poaching

Between the two factories (Pavlova and MG) there was an unwritten agreement that there would be no poaching of qualified tradesmen. These were in short supply, so the free movement from employment in one to work in the other was not allowed.

Many MG employees took for granted that to gain employment in MG you had to know someone there, and have their support in your application. With no such help you would not get a job there.

Peter gained a position at MG in the following way, which satisfied all the conventions: he had been made aware that a position at MG was available, and he had the necessary internal help to support his application. First he terminated his work at Pavlova, and gained a position at Thames Conservancy. At this time it was replacing many of the hand-operated locks with electric ones and this was his job. He held this for about three months, then took the position at MG. He was there from 1968 to 1980.

When a person began at MG there was a two-week period at basic pay while learning the job. When Peter began, on one day he was required to work on fixing a hoist which lowered car bodies onto a trolley, and moved them to where the engine was installed. He worked from 8am to 11pm and was rewarded by only having to work one week at basic rates.

The MG Car Company Canteen – 1937.
(© Oxfordshire County Council, Oxfordshire History Centre)

He was one of six electricians in the Maintenance Section and his work involved electrical installation, such as putting in new plant, lines or buildings, repairing hoists which lifted chassis down from the upper floors, and similar work. Each electrician had a 'mate' to work with.

Peter says that work at MG was purely assembly work and that "nothing was made there, only put together," with the exception of some very small parts. Body parts were made, painted and assembled in Cowley and transported to Abingdon. Only small remedial paint jobs were done here. He notes that the work at Abingdon was never large scale, no big presses as there were in Cowley, and no paint shop. Cars were literally pushed along the assembly lines, which made them a true hand-finished product. The work could have been carried out on any assembly line in the country where there was any spare capacity. The plant did, however, have specialist Research and Development, and Competition Departments. But MG was Abingdon, and leaving it there had senior management support.

Shifts and Breaks

The shift system at MG applied mainly to maintenance people. A shift arrived at 5.30am to start up the plant and the boilers, and get the assembly lines ready to begin the day's work. They also carried out all the necessary maintenance work during their time. This went on until 1.30pm. Another shift took over from 1.30pm until 9.30pm. People worked two weeks in turn on each shift.

The shift system did not involve assembly line workers who simply worked from 7.30am until 4.15pm.

Tea breaks were taken at the place of your work, for example on the assembly lines, with orders for tea and coffee taken by the tea-boys. Lunch was taken in the canteen after the hooter at 1pm. Many employees chose to go home for lunch, and lined up with their bikes at the main gate ready to pour across Marcham Road. Those who ate at work could obtain a main course, the cheapest of which was egg and chips at 1/6d with a pudding of apple pie and custard for 4d.

The canteen was run by a lady called Peggy, who also provided buffets for weddings and other events. She did the buffet for Heather Grant's reception, whose wedding took place in Trinity Church, Abingdon, and the reception was at what was then known as Tatham Hall, which later became Northcourt House, part of Abingdon and Witney College in Northcourt Road.

She recalls that the free drinks at the reception had to stop at 6pm as they were on a very limited budget. Everyone then made their way to the new MG Social Club in Caldecott Road for an evening of dance.

Most of the line-people took the factory holiday in July, but the exceptions were the Goods Inwards and maintenance staff that could carry out necessary repairs during this time. The same was true of tea breaks too, and maintenance men could take the break when they wanted, as a result.

Trades

The difference between a fitter and an electrician was that fitters dealt with anything mechanical, such as replacing and repairing air-lines, air tools, cables on hoists and so on. Electricians alone were qualified to deal with the power supply to lines, and to deal with general electrical installations. If a new building was being put up, MG always used its own maintenance and electrical staff to install the necessary parts.

The Maintenance Section, like other factory sections, held its own festivities, and might book a meal at the Upper Reaches Hotel, or at the MG Social Club in Caldecott Road. Peter Jeffries recalls that the club had a good cricket team, but Peter was not in it.

There were many sports teams in the MG Social Club. Bob Whittington played for the football team in the Oxford Senior League and the Reading Premier League, but the latter required too much travelling. At the beginning MG played in black and white strip, then later played mainly in white. The team was very successful.

Pete says he would not have liked being on the assembly lines, although the money was good. He preferred the variety in his own job, such as on one day, having to drive down to Basingstoke to collect stores from Lansing-Bagnall's when one of their stacker trucks broke down.

No Promotion

At one point the job of electrician foreman came up, and Pete was rather expecting to get it. However, for some reason, it was given to someone fitter but less well qualified than Pete. When another foreman position arose some time later, the process was rather more formal. To end favouritism, proper interviews were held, and this time he was given the job and a new white coat.

The foreman tended to spend more time with management, and his role was to pass down and implement decisions rather than to make those decisions. Other foreman positions were Works Engineer (Doug Garden), Mechanical Foreman (Harold Jones), and a Carpenter Foreman (Hadrian Drewitt).

Dave Mildenhall

Dave worked as a tinsmith at the Cowley Works for many years. His job at one time was to remove dents from painted body shells without damaging the paintwork. To do this he used two tools; a spoon for the outside surface, and a dolly or chaser for the inside. The idea was to work them together and gently and smoothly remove any minor dents.

Chapter 4

FIRE!

Jimmy's Fire

Jimmy Simpson was chief fire officer at MG. He was standing near a store in which were kept padded steering wheels, which replaced the solid Bakelite ones. Somehow this pile began to smoke and spontaneously ignite. Jimmy saw the smoke coming up through the floorboards and, according to others there, he stood and watched in amazement – while the fire alarm was sounding.

Incidentally, Jimmy Simpson's Fire Brigade uniform is occasionally on display at the MG Car Club.

Jimmy Simpson 1st right, and Cyril Cox 3rd from right.

Cyril's Fire

Heidi Reynolds, one of the Abingdon Royal British Legion bar staff, says that her grandfather, Cyril Cox, was a fireman at MG. Cyril also appears in the photo above. Cyril was the only full-time fireman, and his duties included maintaining the equipment, and checking factory fire precautions and fire hazards.

Cyril was deputy to Jimmy Simpson – "More like a foreman" said Roy

Belcher, as he related the following story. It seems that one day smoke began to appear from inside the MG Fire Brigade building. Cyril Cox had been drying his socks in front of an electric fire and they had caught light. On another occasion, some rubber leggings had been put over a heater. The straps melted and went into the heater, which then caught fire. The fire-engine was called out, but not much damage was caused. Unfortunately Cyril's stock of cigarettes which the men could buy was destroyed.

One cause of fire happened more than once. This was at the end of the assembly line where a screw had been carelessly threaded right through electric wiring in an almost finished car, causing it to catch alight.

The men of the Fire Brigade normally worked on the line, or at their usual work, and, rather like lifeboat men, would have to leave this and run to deal with the fire. There were no general fire drills, as such, to disrupt production, but there were competitions between the brigades at the various works factories in Abingdon and in the Midlands, with the aim, of course, of raising standards and keeping up skill levels.

Roy remembers other Fire Brigade members such as Bob Saunders and Arthur Purbrick. Arthur was a D-Day Landings veteran who had received a bullet in the head that day, a bullet which remained in his head for the rest of his life. Arthur shared his carpentry skills with local schools, where he imparted his extensive knowledge to his pupils.

There was an occasion when he was working in the 'black paint shop' and the tannoy sounded the fire alarm; "The Fire Station is on fire." It seems that some toasting bread had caught alight.

Another fire event was when the fire alarm sounded, and the fire engine came round a corner much too fast, and piles of equipment such as helmets and reels of fire hose fell off.

Normally, when a car engine was started up, the exhaust fumes would be taken from the exhaust pipe through a conduit in the factory building and out to the open air. On one occasion someone had either been careless about connecting this, or had forgotten to attach it. In any event, this particular engine was a 'smoker' meaning it gave out thick exhaust smoke. The line was stopped, to the fury of the foreman Dick Stevens. He shouted to get the line started again. The men shouted 'No' because the air there was unbreathable. He retorted that the air was no worse than smoking a cigarette. In what appears to have become a typical MG Works style, one of the men said: "In that case wrap your lips round the exhaust!"

1979 – Barry Parker

Barry Parker worked as required around the factory: on the line, stores, paint shop, and elsewhere. He described the Works as being something of a family, and a bit old-fashioned. He left in 1979.

There was a memorable incident where Barry, while driving an MGB to the paint-shop, took a corner a little too quickly and rammed it into a concrete pillar.

There are stories of fires in the paint-shop itself ... no surprise that smoking was forbidden in the Works. One particular incident occurred while Barry was waiting outside the paint tunnel, to take the next finished vehicle to the outside area. Although the bodies arrived at Abingdon having been painted at

Lessons learned ... no smoking in the workshop.

Pressed Steel, it was often the case that much retouching needed to be done. The first task was to mask off the chrome and windows and so on, then spray the paint. Then the car was pushed into the tunnel where the paint was baked on. It seems that the paint oven in the tunnel became very hot, and paint and petrol in the cars began to boil. However, in this instance, the cause of the fire was the grease and accumulated rubbish on the track. Somehow a fire began, and Barry sounded the alarm for the Works Fire Brigade. The Abingdon Fire Brigade also arrived on the scene, but – not for the first time – the town brigade had arrived before the MG firemen!

The reasons for the delay were probably that the Works Fire Station was near the Main Gate and the distance to the paint tunnel was about 400 yards, while the men also had to change into fire kit and collect extinguishing equipment.

A number of cars were damaged, and their petrol tanks blew up, but fortunately no personnel were injured. When asked later what he was doing when the fire started, Barry replied: "*The Sun* crossword, 5 down!"

Nothing could be done to clear up the resulting mess until the Insurance Assessors had been to complete their work, but then Barry and others were asked to stay late to put things right, and management sent them down coffee and sandwiches to help them along.

One man who did enjoy his job of driving finished cars from the production line to the despatch area, with not too many mishaps, he claims, was Nigel Hawkins, formerly of Spring Road, and now of Tucson Arizona, USA. He and his father-in-law, Gordon Packford, worked at the factory for about 25 years.

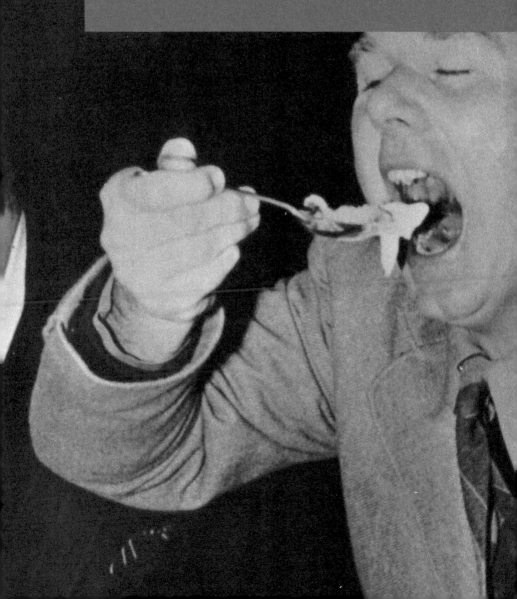

Chapter 5

Some More Characters

In a workforce of around one thousand, there would always be some 'characters,' and some incidents, some of which are described below.

A production worker named Lucy made trims for car seats, and also leather tool bags. Bob Matthews still has one which is extremely well made. During the war she was a gas-welder working on tanks and aircraft, and was so good her work was used as an example for others on how to do it.

Rex Thatcher was 6ft 4in, and big built. According to Vito Orlando, he could pick you up, and walk along with you. This happened to Vito one day when giving an instruction to Rex. Vito was grabbed by his collar and trousers, and carried around the shop floor.

Another prank was when Rex picked up little Ron Smith, and placed him in the boot of an MGB on the line and locked him in. The car was, as usual, lowered down on to the elevated line, with him still in it!

Lowering the chassis – we can only assume that no-one was inside the boot of this car.

Perhaps not by coincidence, Cozy Dixon tells a similar story. On one occasion, men on the line picked him up (he was 18 at the time) and shoved him into an MGB boot. A crane then lifted the car and dumped it on to the lower line – also with him still in it.

Ray Beachey would put plastic bags on his feet and use them as skates round the production line.

Ray Browne of Special Tuning ran a Sunday School at Cothill, and Phil Bolton was sometimes given a lift there in a Mini which had won the Monte Carlo Rally in 1967 or 1968.

'Sailor' Berry was a bare-knuckle boxer, as was 'Stodger' Hudson.

Ralph Tubb was known as 'Harpic' because he was thought to be 'clean round the bend.' His job was to push a four-wheel trolley back to the end of the line, for the next body to be fitted with exhausts from up on the Trim deck, in this case Austin-Healey 3000s. One day an electrician working up on a ladder was in his way. Tubb accidentally knocked him off the ladder and left him dangling in the air until another ladder was provided.

One MG man was landlord of the Prince of Wales pub in Spring Road, known as 'The Steps' – it is now the Abingdon Royal British Legion headquarters. The man was a road-tester, driving newly constructed cars round the Abingdon routes, and on to the railway station to be loaded on to trains. His wife actually ran the pub in the 1950s.

An apprentice was killed in the late 1960s – he had made a go-kart and drove it straight under a truck in the factory grounds. It is said that he was practically beheaded.

An MGB had its top cut off when it ran under a tractor and trailer, just missing the driver's head.

Terry Cheverton had a tracheotomy, and had to wear a tube on his throat to breathe. Nevertheless, he retained his sense of humour, and would play a trick where he would put a plastic bag over his head and pretend to asphyxiate himself. People would panic to get him out but he was breathing through his throat equipment all the time.

Jimmy Cox

When he began at MG in 1945, he told them his name was Sidney, but was told there were enough Sidneys already so he would be called Jimmy, and so it was. He worked at MG for 47 years, beginning as a messenger boy. This enabled him to become familiar with the various departments and to get to know the people there. Later, as a tea-boy, he also began to learn

Jimmy Cox and Percy Standen working on a race engine for the 1955 Le Mans 24-Hour Race.

basic car production, by collecting parts from the stores, and learning the names of the various tools. He also began working on the line, making TC chassis assemblies.

The Assembly Process

In brief, the assembly process was as follows: first the rear springs and axle, and then those at the front were fitted to the bare frame. This was Jimmy Cox's first job. Then the brake cables and pipes were put into place. The wheels were then fitted, and the chassis manually lifted onto the track. This was followed by placing the power unit, then adding the rubber mountings, following which Harry Carter fitted the exhaust system, pedals and handbrake. The chassis was then moved along the line where the bulkhead was installed, together with the petrol pump control box, wiring harness etc. After this the steering column was bolted into place, then came the steering wheel, air cleaner manifold, radiator, brake fluid, and so on. After painting, the chassis was run out of its booth, and one of Jimmy's jobs was to drive these 'rolling chassis' to the main assembly line where the body would be fitted. To do this he had to drive without the benefit of seats or floor. Instead he would stand on the transmission tunnel and operate the pedals as best he could.

By now he could also work as the 'spare man,' even though he was under the normal age for this work. The job required him to perform any assembly task if someone was away from their workplace.

MG was also working on war contracts when Jimmy began there, and he would have helped to construct, among other things, Neptune tanks, which once assembled, were oddly enough sent for scrap, the war being over.

On return from national service in the Far East, he was placed in the development department working with Sid Enever, Alec Hounslow (who had begun as a boy at the Longwall Works in Oxford), Johnny Crook and Harold Wiggins. They were developing a prototype TD model. Jimmy was sent there initially to help repair this after it had been involved in a crash and needed to be rebuilt. Alec Hounslow claimed that the crash had been caused by failure of a steering arm, but the evidence was inconclusive.

Thus began his career in the development department, where his first major role was to work on BMC B-Series power units for the MGA prototypes, which had been entered for the 1955 Le Mans competition. There was a big accident in this race, people were killed and injured, and the MG car was destroyed.

He became Chairman of the Staff Union, which was an organisation for those who did not wish to join the Amalgamated Engineering Union, and was apparently very well thought of. He says that not once did he go on strike. Indeed MG is said to be the only BMC factory never to have gone out on strike. Or was it …? Brian Salsbury tells a different story, later on … (see Chapter 6).

Jimmy went to the MG facility and race-track at Dundrod in County Armagh, Northern Ireland, to try out B-Series engines. Later the competition department was moved over to BMC. Jimmy continued to work on the EX179 and EX181, which led to him travelling to Salt Lake City, USA with the team.

Gus Thomas can be seen on the far left.

Faith Healer

Gus Thomas was the grandfather of Brian Moylan's wife. Gus was well known as a faith healer, but Jimmy was sceptical. However, a time came when he was employed on polishing cylinder heads. This was very dusty work and he did it in a shed outside of the main workshops. Although Jim wore scarf and mask, he developed a frozen shoulder. Nothing could get rid of it so he finally went to Gus Thomas to ask what he could do. Gus said nothing but placed his hands close to but not on Jimmy's shoulders and moved his hands up and down without actually touching. Jimmy says he could feel warmth in his shoulders, and the pain almost completely disappeared.

Another case was Brian Hillier who suffered from back trouble. This caused him to walk slightly bent, and possibly had disc trouble. He went to a specialist, Fricker in London, who simply told Hillier to throw has stick away. The man did so and could walk normally again.

Jimmy no longer doubts this ability.

Jimmy Cox (far right) with the development team and the EX181 at Utah in 1959. Also seen here is driver Phil Hill (middle), between George Eyston and Alec Hounslow.

"Take That!"

Jimmy tells a story where, because of his love of football, he was in the habit of giving a good kick to any loose cardboard box which he found in his way. He did this a little too heartily one day, and the box flew up and struck Cecil Wheeler on the side of the head. Instinctively, according to him, Cecil struck Jimmy a strong blow in the stomach and knocked him down and winded him. Usually this would have been a dismissal offence, but Jack Lewis the charge-hand, who was nearby, saw what had happened and they all treated it as 'horse-play', once Jimmy told them he was OK.

When MG finally closed in 1980, Jimmy went to Cowley, working on

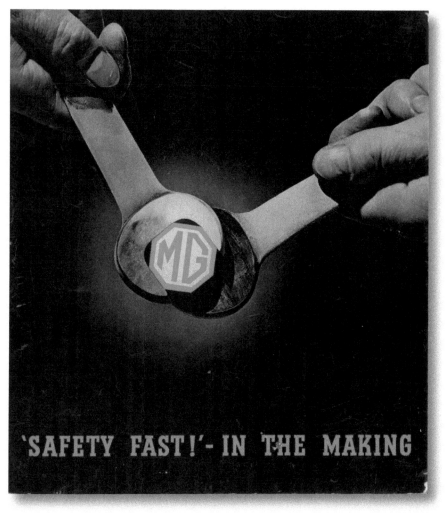

the Honda Ballade, and later was appointed project engineer on the MG Maestro and MG Montego.

Rod Clewley

Rod emailed me with the information that both his parents (Horace and Doris, née Silvester) worked at MG in the 1930s. Doris was a typist and was in the office when the logo 'SAFETY FAST' was first conceived. She remembers such names there as Cecil Kimber, Harry Rummins (Doris and Horace's Best Man), George Probert and Reg Ingram.

Rod played cricket and hockey for the MG clubs in the '50s and '70s.

'Animal Crackers'

Peter Thouless worked at MG, as did his son Tony, and he tells a tale of Jim Heskett who one day walked across from the main gate to a smallholding on the other side of the road, to feed the horses. On the way in he was kicked in the rear by a horse, and on the way out was bitten in exactly the same place by a donkey. He felt very embarrassed having to reveal his injuries to the Works' nurse.

The surgery was managed efficiently by Nurse Goodenough and, before her, the very strict Nurse Budden. It seems that there was always a

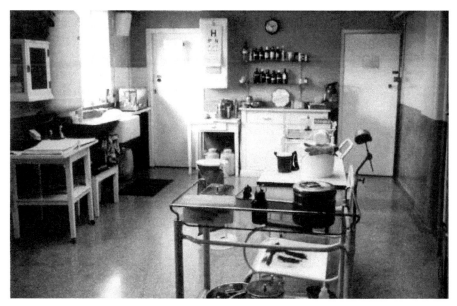

The MG surgery in the 1970s.

queue waiting outside. Interestingly, Nurse Goodenough, during the war years, had worked with Sir Archibald McIndoe, the famous surgeon who pioneered facial skin grafts, working at East Grinstead with injured RAF crewmen who had suffered severe burns in air crashes.

Tim Cairns

Tim worked straight from the beginning on the Trim Deck carrying out various jobs, each of which was timed for around ten minutes. He would fit wire-looms front and back, and steering columns among other things. The job often only took six minutes in order for the operatives to finish early, and if it ever took more than the six minutes some would complain to the foreman, as they wanted to get the job done and finished.

Starting at 7.30am, often they would finish around 3pm and sit there, their day's allocation complete, and relax and maybe play cards until 4.30pm, the official leaving time.

Some went a little further than relaxing. Under his workbench, out of sight of authority, Cozy Dixon had fitted up a special cupboard with pillows, and only those who worked nearby would know that he was sleeping there behind the doors and out of sight until 4.30 came round.

One unpleasant job on the Trim Deck was glueing of seat covers. The area was fairly closed in, so those working there would be sniffing glue fumes all day. Tim remembers seeing men with silly grins on their faces as a result, and complaining of headaches. Eventually the situation was rectified for clear health reasons.

Time Out

Tim mentions the discipline of MG. Some say it was relaxed, but others say it could be quite brutal. If you were late, you could be 'quartered,' meaning that you would lose fifteen minutes' pay. If this happened three times in a month, you would receive a warning that next time you would be suspended for one day. If you were late again, you would have a day's suspension. And then, if late again, you would receive warning of a three-day suspension so that if you dared again to be late, you would indeed be suspended without pay for three days.

At that time, in his teenage years, Tim and his friends played in pop-music bands, and one particular weekend they were hoping to perform in Swansea and Neath. The journey would take them seven or eight hours, so they wanted to leave early from work on the Friday.

To do this they planned to work the suspension system and receive suspensions for Friday, Monday and Tuesday. It all went according to plan and finally they came in on the Thursday, and received their three days punishment. However, the management knew what the boys were up to, and gave some of them suspensions for Friday, Monday and Tuesday, but others the Monday, Tuesday and Wednesday. This rather put the great plan in difficulties but, as Tim says, they took the Friday off anyway.

At the Social Club, the band would often play at a weekend, occasionally

Friends and colleagues – members of the Service Department in 1952.

with Cozy Dixon as an extra percussionist. There was a good family atmosphere there, and Tim recalls very little drunken behaviour. It was perfectly normal for people working on the line to socialise with foremen and middle management, and there was very little 'us and them.' Senior management were rarely seen however.

Alfie
Tim recalls a character named Alfie from Marcham. One night at the Social Club Alfie took on a bet that he could consume fifty raw eggs placed in beer glasses – shades of the Paul Newman film *Cool Hand Luke*. It was all fine until the final glass when he really looked as if the whole lot would reappear, so the crowd rapidly backed away from the stage. But he did manage it and won the bet.

Percy Harwood
Percy was a line-sweeper, performing this task for the last two years before his retirement. Every Friday he would come to Tim's workstation and Tim would give him £5 to hold for him for the week. It would be returned to Tim on the Thursday so he'd have some beer money for Thursday night, and pay-day would be the next day.

He was entirely trustworthy it seems, because on one Thursday he did not arrive to give Tim the weekly fiver. Eventually Percy's wife turned up, frantic with worry and gave Tim his cash. It seems Percy had become ill so couldn't get to work, and was very concerned that he had to give Tim his money as usual.

Chapter 6

More on the Unions

Sporting the blue overalls specific to factory workers.

Working together

According to some accounts, with regard to management and trade unions, it was very much them and us, although there was little open warfare at the Abingdon site. That tended to happen elsewhere. Union activity mainly manifested itself in such things as rate-fixing and payment for unusual work. If the factory ran out of wire wheels for instance, they carried on making cars with the cheaper disc wheels. Then, at a later date, the cars that should have had wire wheels had to be reworked to the correct specification, and of course this was not a case of simply changing the wheels; it was the whole suspension and hubs at the front and the axles at the back.

The main Union (TGWU) shop steward was Eric Brind from Drayton, who was considered to be good at this job. Most people generally got on well with management. Senior foremen wore white coats, the others green ones. Workers wore blue overalls.

MG had always been a 'closed shop,' meaning that everyone had to belong to one of the trade unions; 'no union membership – no job.' This system is now unlawful of course. As an alternative there was the Staff Association, which represented those working in the various offices, rather than directly on the assembly of vehicles. Its representative was Jimmy Cox.

In later years there were three unions: the TGWU (Transport and General Workers' Union) with Senior Convenor Eric Brind, AUEW (Amalgamated Union of Engineering Workers) and NUVB (The National Union of Vehicle Builders) under Jack Adams.

No Case to Answer

Stuart Jackson had been towing a caravan with a Vanden Plas Princess, when a car ran into the passenger side, and both cars were seriously damaged. Stuart and the other driver had to attend Dartford Magistrates Court. At the hearing, the driver of the other car said he could not see the relevant driver in court – he had mistaken Stuart's co-driver (Derek Argyle, who was fortunately not sitting in the passenger seat at the time of the collision) as the actual driver, and this man was not in court. Finally the case was dismissed for lack of evidence.

'Under pressure' – the '60s were a turbulent time for car manufacturers following the changes from BMC, BMH and BLMC. Pictured: abandoned pressure gauge following the closure of MG.

What made Stuart particularly angry was that his union, the NUVB, refused to help with the costs of the case, or of legal advice and assistance, because Stuart had not paid a political levy earlier. The MG company paid these, and even provided a driver and car to take him to Dartford Court.

The matter was not helped by the fact that Stuart could not leave the NUVB, because then he would not be in a union, and could not therefore remain as an employee, so had to take it. Stuart eventually became Special Tuning stores foreman after the death of George Hubbard.

MGB Lines Restarted

Industrial relations were not always cosy at the Abingdon Works, but usually problems were dealt with quickly. Disruptions to work tended to be the result of strikes elsewhere, although one exception occurred in 1963, when some men walked out after suspension by management.

An example of a stoppage because of a strike elsewhere occurred in 1966. Three lines at Abingdon had been halted since the 10th of May 1966, as a result of a lack of engines from the Longbridge Austin Works, and production of 700 cars had been lost. This was caused by a strike

Abingdon factory roller test – part of the end of production tests and inspections.

at Longbridge, due to some men demanding to be taken on after having been listed for redundancy.

Some Abingdon workers had been put on non-assembly work. The Midget, Austin-Healey Sprite, and Austin-Healey 3000 production lines were all working normally.

Again in 1966, a two-week strike at Morris Radiators disrupted MG Works production, after 450 men had been laid off. Four MGB lines at Abingdon had been idle for 2½ days the previous week, and were then closed altogether until further notice. There was a shortage of exhaust systems, oil coolers and petrol tanks, nor were there any Sprite engines coming to Abingdon from Coventry.

The Wheels Come Off

Brian Salsbury worked on the MGB line, and says that he once caused a one-day strike at Abingdon Works. It seems that he fitted a steering wheel to a vehicle and the inspectors passed it as satisfactory. Later, on its test run, the steering wheel suddenly parted company with the car. A complaint was made and Brian was suspended. His trade union called the men out, and Brian was reinstated shortly after.

1974-75 – The Three-Day Week

As a result of high inflation and rising prices, many industries, but especially the miners, felt they deserved a wage-increase to counter this. A miners' strike was eventually called, and this led to a severe shortage of coal to maintain electricity supplies. The government felt unable to import expensive coal because of the balance of payments problem.

To conserve supplies, the government announced a three-day working week from January until March 1974. TV companies had to stop broadcasting at 10.30pm.

At one point during the Three-Day Week the MG factory had all its lights on one morning, but the hospital next door had none. The union was not happy with this, so they complained to management and threatened a strike if the situation was not altered. The men were told that the hospital was on a different circuit, but they didn't believe this. Down went the tools. Soon after this the situation was rectified, the hospital lights were turned on and unnecessary MG lights turned off. This story came from Tony Thouless.

Chapter 7

Suspicious Behaviour at MG

The Dark Side – Pilfering 'Rife' at MG

It is perhaps inevitable that there would be a darker side of things, and so, among the excitement and the success, stories such as that which follows would appear in the local press. But there were no more and no less of these stories than in other workplaces, and it all helps to fill in the bigger picture.

In 1929, Frederick Bartlett and Gertrude Bartlett were charged with stealing a 12-volt dynamo worth £9.17.6d, the property of MG Motor Company at the Pavlova Works. It was identified by John Henry Reed, the MG chief storekeeper.

Fred Hemmins, a car-cleaner, said in his testimony that while he was mending a road there, he saw Frederick Bartlett with a bundle under an arm, wrapped in blue rag. The accused took the bundle to the back of the Works then returned without it. Later it was found that it had been laid in some grass. Hemmins then reported the matter. Another employee, Richard Ellis, said that he then kept watch on a field at the back of the Works, and saw Gertrude Bartlett with a man and a young girl going along a path leading from Marcham Road to Shippon Road, which skirts the MG premises. They stopped where he knew the dynamo to be, then went towards Shippon. Later he saw them return. The woman picked up the dynamo, then was joined by the man and girl. They all went towards Marcham Road, then he saw the man go into the 'White Horse' pub, and later catch up with Bartlett and the girl in Caldecott Road. They all sat by the river, the woman carrying the dynamo, and he sent for the police.

PC Garrett went to the river and saw the group. He asked the woman where she got the dynamo, and he asked her to accompany him to the police station where she was detained.

Frederick Bartlett was brought in later. The man said he was not guilty, and the woman said she had thought the rag would be useful for her grate.

Both decided to be dealt with summarily, but Fred Bartlett was remanded in custody for further inquiries.

On another occasion, the *Herald* newspaper ran a headline announcing that pilfering was rife at MG. John W----, a maintenance worker of Kingston Bagpuize, was fined a total of £95, pleading guilty to stealing petrol worth 8/- and tools valued at £24.13.3d. Several others were involved over a long period. W---'s offence was discovered as he made to leave through the gate, and was stopped by a security man at 10pm on January the 14th 1966. W---'s home was later searched, and

The Marcham Road entrance guard gate.

other items found. Mr W--- was a married man with three children, and previously had a good work record over ten years.

Easy Pickings

Several contributors recalled that pilfering was a problem, but this was probably true of most large organisations. Working in an atmosphere that stocks every component necessary to make a car, it was not surprising that some people tried to smuggle parts out. In the 1960s and 1970s, cars were very low tech – an ignition coil was an ignition coil, and would fit and function in almost any make of car. These days things are very much more specific to a particular model, even within the same make. At that time, however, a Sprite or a Midget used the BMC A-Series engine, which was also fitted to the Morris Minor/Austin A40 or the first Minis, need I say more. So, quite naturally, the factory security officers would be on duty at each gate as the workers arrived and left work, to keep an eye out for bulging bags or pockets. Heather Grant describes some of

82

the security men as "obnoxious and over-bearing" and too ready to play the "Big I Am." Not all of them, though; the father of Andy Glass, who worked at MG and later set up in his own business, was considered to be 'OK.'

Other incidents, for example, were where a worker would wrap a battery in Christmas wrapping and walk through the gate with it, fooling the guards, or where a man tried to smuggle Bluecol anti-freeze out in a Thermos Flask.

On another Christmas occasion, a man wrapped a propshaft part in wrapping paper, and placed the top of a Christmas tree in such a way that it looked like he was carrying home a fir-tree.

As would be expected in such an environment, the tradition of practical jokes was strongly in evidence. When someone parked his bike in a cycle shed, some boys strung it up from the ceiling so he couldn't find it. Welding someone's boots to the floor if they stood talking for too long was almost normal. One lad, apparently a sweeper, was shoved in a dustbin just as management came round. The boys had to keep their fingers crossed nothing would be heard until the white coats had gone.

Look For Yourself!

On one noteworthy day, which has passed into MG folklore, there was a new guard on duty at the main Marcham Road gate, which at the present time would have stretched exactly between McDonald's and the new police station (the picture opposite was taken just a week before they demolished this gate). Straight across the road is the current Ock Mill restaurant, but in the '60s/'70s this was a listed building, and one of the MG inspectors rented it with his wife, and kept pigs in the back yard. (There was an army of grey-coated inspectors overseeing every stage of production, and noting down on each car's individual record card every pass or fail at every stage of assembly, saying maybe that the axle was noisy, or noting that there was a cross-threaded screw in the gearlever chrome surround.)

This inspector who was, to be kind, pretty rotund, possibly around 25 stone, used to visit the canteen at close-of-play every day to collect the waste food for his pigs, which he collected in one of those water-carrier type massive galvanised drums on wheels. As everyone queued at the closed gate, waiting for the guard to let them go at the sound of the hooter, this new guard spotted the chap with the 20 gallons of pigswill, and asked what was in the drum. Not satisfied with the inevitable answer he asked:

"How can I be sure that's only pigswill?" Next thing he was ankle-deep in it with the inspector remarking: "Have a … look for yourself!"

Vito Orlando recalls that one man wore a very long overcoat to and from work, and used to hang a steering rack round his neck. He would do up the coat and walk out of the factory.

Another dodge was to have a bike with a basket – put a car battery in and cover it and ride out.

Incidentally, Vito had a renaming experience like Jimmy Cox's. When he first arrived he said his name was Vito and he was told they couldn't handle that – "From now on you're called Victor" – and so it became.

Brian Wood

There were other forms of criminality going on too, and not just in the MG factory.

In the 1970s and 1980s Brian was a Detective Sergeant with the Thames Valley Police Motor Vehicle Investigation Squad, and in those days MGs were a favourite of car thieves.

The car thieves knew all about engine and chassis-numbers, but what they did not know was that MG was one of the few manufacturers who stamped and recorded gearbox numbers. Brian spent many hours checking the MG records for gearbox numbers, which, if his memory served him correctly, were kept in metal-bound ledgers.

Stolen vehicle squads throughout the UK, and even from overseas, would send their requests for gearbox number checks to Brian, and the records were meticulous. Thanks to these records, hundreds of stolen MG cars were recovered and restored to their rightful owners, and the thieves duly convicted.

Little SUS1E

Another story Brian narrates concerns dodgy tax-discs. "In 1966 I was a Detective Sergeant with the Thames Valley Police Stolen Vehicle Squad. I left the office at Cumnor to go to my bank at Botley. I parked in the car park next to an MGB and as I walked past I noticed it had the personalised registration number of SUS1E. As is my wont, I looked at the tax disc and noted it had been crudely altered. I checked with the Police National Computer which showed that the number of SUS1E had not been issued.

"Ten minutes later a happy young couple, all full of the delights of life, approached the car, holding hands. They looked just the part to have an open top sports car. A few questions later they were in the back of my police car, and on their way to St Aldate's police station. Their carefree attitude had diminished somewhat.

"The car had been stolen from Leeds, so they were charged and bailed to Leeds Magistrates Court, and were later convicted of the car's theft.

"Interestingly the couple's parents were headmaster and headmistress, respectively, of public schools in Leeds. It's a pity they had not installed a sense of responsibility into their offspring.

"Incidentally, the girl's name was Susie."

Possibly the intended lifestyle of SUS1E's occupants ...

Brian recalls: "On one occasion I was asked to go and fill a bottle with oil. A foreman, Fred Wale, spotted this and told me: 'We don't do that here!' It seems that unknown to me at the time, the oil was being stolen."

1979 MG Club Stabbing
In 1979, the MG club was the site of a stabbing incident. Three local men arrived at the club claiming that B…. owed money to a friend of one of the three. There was a good deal of pushing, shoving and threatening behaviour.

Later the group moved to the MG car park and this is where B...., the man who was said to owe the money, himself made threats to the three. Witnesses reported that this same man 'went berserk' and stabbed one of the three with a carving knife.

The incident was reported to the police, and later the man with the knife was placed at a secret address until the trial. Incidentally, he became married whilst there.

At the trial, the knife wielder was found not guilty of grievous bodily harm with intent, while one of the other people involved was bound over to keep the peace in the sum of £100.

Tony Thouless was witness to the distressing occurrence in 1979.

The whole incident was reported in the *Herald*, although actual names have been omitted here. Among witnesses to the incident were Tony Thouless, who was captain of the MG shooting team, and his wife, and John Struggles, all of whom had been hoping for a quiet evening in the club.

You Bet!

One man on a line took bets for the men and later went with these to a bookie's. At the time, this was all illegal. Until the Betting and Gaming Act of 1960, betting could only take place at the racecourse or at a turf-accountant's – or bookie's – premises. To do the latter you had to set up a credit account and have a telephone. These rules effectively, and perhaps deliberately, excluded most working people. Bookies got round this by having 'runners' who would go from the betting shop to private houses and workplaces, and take bets in return for a commission. This was illegal, too, and the sight of a runner being chased by a constable was not so unusual. One day a lorry driver came to the Works – in fact a tax inspector in disguise – and found out who was taking the bets.

One legal form of gambling was where you could select a number, pay your entrance fee, and if your number came up, you won the cash. Rather like football draws in pubs today.

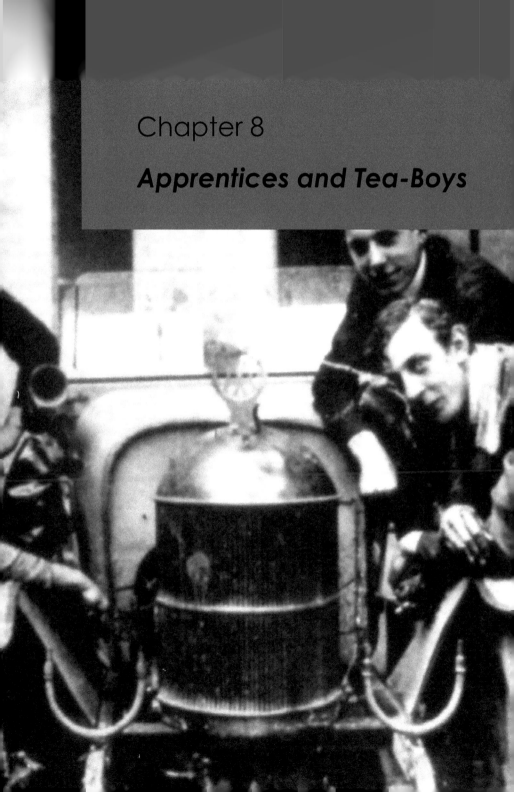

Chapter 8

Apprentices and Tea-Boys

In the prewar period there were no apprentices, but there were a number of tea-boys. They were of some importance because, as Frank 'Dutchy' Holland recalled, some 60 years later, there were no reliefs for absent assembly workers, so this was done by the tea-boys. He recalls that on the various lines there were: Percy Hudson, whose father Jimmy was a sweeper, Dutchy Holland and Stan Withers on the Chassis Line, Les Morse and Mrs Didcock the sweeper on the Body Line, and on Service there was Vic Pratley and Jack Woodmore. This is just a few of them. Other tea-boys included Syd Cox and Jock Denton.

Peter Neal

Peter Neal studied maths and science at the Abingdon Institute of Further Education in Conduit Road – as did Peter Jeffries (whose story was told earlier in Chapter 3) – and recalls wearing the college black tie with red stripes, which he still possesses.

At this time Peter Neal, MG's first postwar apprentice, came to work with Jimmy Cox. One of Jimmy's tricks was to dismantle a gear box, jumble up the parts and tell Peter to reassemble it. If he could, he would have no trouble with engine work, and so it proved. All the apprentices who worked with Jimmy went through this.

Peter tells a story of his five-year apprenticeship in the Drawing Office, during which he realised that much of his work was to act as 'gopher' to the more senior people there. His pay at that time was £2.1.4d a week, which was carefully counted out for him at the Wages Office. His rent in South Avenue was partly paid by his Dad.

One person for whom Peter ran around was Terry Mitchell, a draughtsman who was an habitual pipe-smoker, but because he spent most of his money building model railways at home, he had little for anything else. Peter remembers him forever knocking out that pipe and relighting it. He would regularly ask Peter to go to a local shop in Spring Road to buy one ounce of 'Cut Golden Bar' tobacco, and matches and pipe-cleaners costing 2/11/2d. The first time this happened, Peter went by bicycle and, trying to get through main gate security, was told he could not go out ("Oi! Where are you going?"). He was told to get a Pass.

The second time, Peter learned that he did not need a Pass if he made out he was simply going to the Top Office (by the Cemetery Road exit). All it needed was for him to wave a blank piece of paper, and he could get through security. Of course this only worked if he walked, rather than taking his bike, so it took longer but was a lot less problematic.

Roy Belcher

Roy attended the Council School in Conduit Road, and joined MG in 1954, after completing his National Service with 40 Field Regiment Royal Artillery in Germany. He stayed for 26 years, only leaving when the Works closed in 1980. "MG enabled me to buy a house, have a good job, and be married with three children."

Other Belchers at MG were his father, Bill, on inspection in the Finishing Department, and Dave (no relation) who fitted rear axles on the Austin-Healey 3000. Terry Belcher, who was a near relation, worked in the paint-shop. This was a small operation because the car bodies were made at Pressed Steel Oxford, and painted, then delivered to Abingdon.

If there had been rain, the bodies would need to be dried off before being sent upstairs to Trim Deck, where the cars were moved along on trolleys for fitting with electrics, some upholstery, etc. Then they were lowered to the elevated track (elevated so men could work under *and* over it), then to floor level, then driven out.

Roy's work hours were generally 8am to 6pm, and piece-work allowed them to complete their quotas and clock out. Overtime, when available, was from 6pm to 8pm.

In 1954 he was working on the Magnette line, where, for example, he fitted the wiring loom and connected the electrics. He moved in 1956 to the front of the line, fitting the wooden dash fascia panels. One of his many and varied jobs at the Works was on Rectification, once the road tests were completed. This was where cars which had shown some minor defect were bought back to the factory to have the fault corrected.

Some vehicles would be driven around the test routes, and those for export driven to the station.

Roy relates that certain test engines were run without oil until they stopped, to see how long they could last. He says the sound and the smell were horrific.

For a long time Eddie Dixon (husband of Iris) was Roy's foreman on the assembly line, working on the Sprite and Midget lines. "It was like a big family" says Roy. He spent a record 18 years as relief man on the MG A, Austin-Healey 3000, and MGB lines. A relief man, as explained elsewhere, was an experienced worker who could take the position of

somebody who was absent, and could be required to perform any job.

Roy particularly remembers the day the Works finally closed down, because it also happened to be his wedding anniversary, 31st October 1980.

Another story told to me by Jimmy Cox was when they were testing the EX181 experimental car (nicknamed 'The Roaring Raindrop') at Abingdon Airfield runway. Firstly, a problem arose when they tried to drive it out of the Development Department, as there was only limited space to move the car out of there, and very limited movement of the steering wheel, as the car was designed to move only in a straight line for speed trials. This involved a great deal of pushing it back and forth with a tiny amount of leeway each time. Vito, who happened to be the

Pushing and pulling was clearly an inherent part of preparations for the Roaring Raindrop.

same size as Stirling Moss and Phil Hill, for whom the seating was designed, was invited to sit at the wheel during this exercise, and, after a great deal of effort, it was finally parked in the Finishing Department just where they wanted it.

On a separate occasion, at the RAF Abingdon runway, filming the car for television after the record-breaking effort at Utah, Jimmy was driving it, and, according to Roy, Jimmy forgot the steering wheel had very limited movement; Jimmy describes how the wheels dug into soft soil and the car ended upside down, but with little damage to him or to the car. The EX181 was sent to BMC's works at Coventry for rebuilding.

It's interesting to note that there are some today who still believe that this car was really Malcolm Campbell's Bluebird.

When Phil Hill broke the Land Speed Record for that class of engine in Salt Lake City, Utah, the announcement was made to MG workers over the tannoy loudspeaker system.

There was a vibrant Developments Department at Abingdon. Keith Faulkner and Geoff Clarke occasionally travelled to the Motor Industry Research Association near Nuneaton, testing (often to destruction) various

The crash test was an essential prerequisite for exporting MGs into the US market.

new parts which were being experimented upon. This had a banked race track, with areas where a Belgian pavé (very rough cobbled ground) could be used for testing various parts being tried out. Cars would be tested almost to destruction here. Also the drivers – if a man drove too long on the pavé he could seriously damage his back and kidneys, as well as the vehicle. This happened to a man driving an Austin-Healey 3000, but the man recovered.

A dynamometer for measuring mechanical power of cars was often used. Some foreign cars would be sent for testing there – one Japanese model was found to exhibit exactly the same parts and identity as an Austin-Healey – a copy.

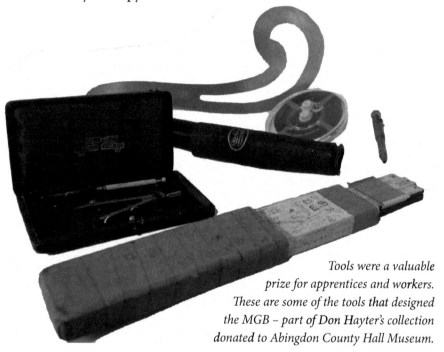

Tools were a valuable
prize for apprentices and workers.
These are some of the tools that designed
the MGB – part of Don Hayter's collection
donated to Abingdon County Hall Museum.

Cars and their modifications might be tested on 'C' Circuit (C for Cotswolds) which was around Birdlip near Gloucester, or the V8 Circuit around Lake Bala in Wales, to try out on the steep mountain roads there.

One job was changing the EX181 so that it ran on petrol rather than on methanol; if the latter blew up there was no visible explosion, unlike the yellow flash of a petrol explosion. Methanol had been used because it gave more output; the more you put through the carburettor, with the same amount of oxygen, the more energy you got.

One problem was the USA demanding ever more modifications for imported cars, for example provision of airbags, crash-testing at the concrete crash barrier at Abingdon with crash-dummies, cameras on board, and so on. Mike Hearn and Roy Brocklehurst were the main people dealing with US modification requirements – both worked in Developments.

Geoff Clarke

At the end of school, Geoff had decided he liked cars and would like to work with them. He applied to MG and began in August 1959 as a tea-boy, and later applied to be an apprentice. He needed to be 16 for this. This change of status was a normal route to apprenticeships apparently. He attended an interview with Mr Gardner and Tom Nicholls (apprentice supervisor), and sat exams in maths and English, etc., at the Technical College in Conduit Road close to Conduit Road school. He passed these, and then began in the Tool Store as was usual. Geoff recalls that this had a blast-proof concrete structure inside, from the war, and the store contained lots of wartime tools for tanks etc. It is probable that apprentices worked in the Tools Store first, so they became familiar with what they and others would be using.

After three months or so, he was reassigned to the Drawing Office for the same length of time. Then came the assembly line to learn the work of the factory. At the same time he was on day-release to college, first at Bury Street School and then Northcourt Road (North Berks College of Further Education) undergoing annual assessments, and advice on improvement if needed. Geoff won a book prize for being best apprentice of the 2nd Year, and later also won a still smart-looking set of tools (inscribed) for being best in the 4th year. Apprentices always wore scarf, shirt and black and red tie to college. At the end of the apprenticeship they could choose which department to work in, but could not insist on that choice. Geoff went for Development, where his first job in fact was on the experimental EX181, with Frankie Dalton, a fitter.

As apprentices they would be sent away on courses to gain experience and self-confidence. Some of these places were: BMC's Coventry engine plant, Tractor and Transmissions and SU Carburettors, both in Birmingham, with management training at Haseley Manor, Warwick, the BMC conference centre and training establishment. Here they learned personal confidence by giving talks and speeches, by gaining management skills and so on.

Development Department

Geoff Clarke spent most time in Development with Jimmy Cox. This department consisted of the Drawing Office and the Development shop below the stairs, in which resided Jimmy and his engines and gearboxes, plus six other men. Jimmy also worked on experimental cars, where newly designed parts would be tested and modified as necessary to see if they were suitable. Examples of parts might be a modified gearbox, pedal box system or anything else. They used a dynamometer to measure engine energy output (brake horsepower) and the effectiveness of modifications.

At one point, when testing at MIRA (Nuneaton), cars were going round at 130mph on the banked circuit, and it was found the tread was being stripped off the tyres. A complaint was made to Dunlop, the tyre manufacturers. It seems that the tyres were not designed for such high speeds, and so more suitable ones were substituted.

An incident occurred when a car was on this same circuit and, as was often the case, some crows were flying about over part of the route. One crow seriously misjudged its flight and smashed into the windscreen, went right through it, shot between the two drivers, and landed in the back of the car. Both drivers were okay, but badly shaken up. Neither felt able to drive that route again.

Rag Week

Rag Week was a series of events run by AERE and MG apprentices who attended North Berkshire College of Further Education in Northcourt Road. The idea was to raise money for local charities, such as Tesdale and Bennett House Schools for Handicapped Children. There would be a Rag Queen, and in 1969 this was 21-year-old Pat Butler. The events would begin with carol singing in the Market Place, then a float parade, Viking ship, pram race, races in dustbins and baths on wheels, and pub-crawls. There would be a barbecue on Ock Meadow, and entertainment by local pop-groups. For some reason the event was called the 'M.U.R.K.' (though they cannot remember what this stood for). On one occasion they climbed up on to the advertising board at front of the 'Regal' cinema, and replaced the name of the advertised film there with a sheet bearing the word 'MURK' in large letters.

Tim Davies

This is Tim's story of how he obtained his apprenticeship. He recalls the time in 1978, climbing the narrow wooden stairway up to the Drawing Office

Hard at work in the Drawing Office in 1961. Quarter scale model in foreground.
(Courtesy MG Car Club, Abingdon)

with plenty of apprehension for a formal interview in front of a panel chaired by Chief Engineer, Don Hayter. A daunting experience, he recalls, and only one leading question; was he passionate about mechanical engineering and cars? He answered; "Yes," which was Tim being economical with the truth.

He didn't dare tell them that he was there just because he found Technical Drawing pretty easy at school, and the MG factory was just up the road from his parents' house.

Tim recalls that he was one of the last of the MG apprentices. Tim completed his first year of training school at the BL Body plant, Oxford, then transferred to the Abingdon works in Summer 1978. He remained there beyond closure, as the Drawing Office was working on the Honda Bounty project. He then transferred back to Cowley in 1981.

On that first day, secretary May Saunders ushered him into Mr Hayter's office, and it was he who guided Tim around, introducing him to staff along the way. Tim was struck by the contrast between this musty 'living museum,' which appeared to be little changed since MG had moved to Abingdon in

1929, and the airy modern technical training school in Cowley, where he had spent the previous year.

He met Terry Mitchell, who was head of the chassis design department where Tim was placed. He was the archetypical old-time engineer, chugging away on his pipe. He was passionate about his work. Tim later learned that, when not designing at MG, Terry spent his spare hours in his home workshop, creating scale models of steam locomotives from original drawings and raw materials. Terry placed Tim under the wing of jovial Bob Staniland, who very quickly put him at his ease.

After a quick chat, Bob laid out a couple of drawings for Tim to look over. Huge, and far more complex than anything he had previously encountered. Tim was at first daunted. After a few minutes, however, he was able to decipher and begin to understand some of the detail. One thing that struck him was the columns of beautifully hand-printed notes, describing everything from the material and finish specifications, to all the manufacturing instructions and test standards applicable to the component.

He was asked; "How is your printing?"

"We always use stencils" Tim admitted.

"We don't use stencils here; best you get some practice."

Consequently, Tim's earliest memory of life in the MG Design Office was spending many hours freehand printing notes copied from a technical manual.

By the end of that week, Tim was fairly pleased with his endeavours. All text five millimetres tall (give or take), evenly spaced and consistently(ish) sloped. Tim was deemed proficient enough to make simple modifications to the drawings. When these modifications were completed the drawing was taken to the print room, where Pauline or Linda would run it through the blueprint machine to copy. The eye-watering stench of ammonia was overpowering, and Tim could never understand how the 'poor girls' could spend eight hours in there every day.

Checking the Drawings

Bob would then spread out the checking print on a layout table, and ceremoniously sharpen his red and yellow pencils. Yellow for good, red for bad. After poring over the drawing, much contemplation and some rigorous scribbling, the marked-up print and original drawing would be presented back to Tim for correction, or to redo notes which weren't considered sufficiently neat.

It was only a matter of weeks later when Don Hayter emerged from his office and gathered everyone together. He announced that the British Leyland Group were henceforth to scan every engineering drawing for archiving on microfiche. To ensure consistent legibility, forthwith all text on drawings must be produced by stencil.

One fond recollection was that apprentices would spend time in various departments, chosen according to their planned career, observing and participating in the daily routines.

Tim was a potential design draughtsman, and spent some time on the production line. For six weeks he would spend half a day with each operator on B Line, initially just watching, but by the end of the shift ideally he would be able to complete each task before the shout went up, and the car was pushed along the track to the next station.

There could be three or so operators at each stage, so he got to know them pretty well, and they seemed to enjoy having a 'sprog' to do the more menial tasks, or even the whole job for them, as he gained confidence and gradually got the 'knack.'

It was a noisy environment, he recalls. As well as the regular clunkings and bangings there was always plenty of banter, yelling, singing and so on. One particular day when working on the elevated section he became aware that this banter was following a common topic. With regular 'Yeehahs!' and bursts of 'Whip crack away!' amongst others, there appeared to be some sort of ongoing cowboy theme.

Around mid-morning Tim made his excuses to go to the toilet (ie, have a cigarette). Smoking was permitted in the factory, but only behind an iron railing next to the stores. As he leaned over the rail dragging on a Number 6, he happened to glance down. There, attached to the heels of his safety boots with double-sided tape, was a large pair of riding spurs made from sponge rubber. The penny dropped!

He attempted to push them off but was obviously being watched. A huge cheer went up from the shop floor, followed by a rousing chorus of *Like a Rhinestone Cowboy*, and a young apprentice turned a particularly burning shade of scarlet.

Tim Feels Faint

There could be stranger experiences even than that. Tim describes how the high point of an MG apprenticeship was always a spell in the 'glamorous' Motorsport department. On his first day, there were cars

TR-7 V8 rally car in action, circa 1977.

being delivered back from a rally the previous weekend. Battered, dented and filthy, the roar from the supercharged V8 engines was deafening, and echoed around the workshop as the TR-7s limped into the work bays. Somehow the boot of one car had become caked on the inside with dried-on mud. Presented with a scrubbing brush, sponge, bucket of water and cleaning spray solution, Tim began his task. Keen to make a good initial impression, he attacked the job with gusto, and spent a good twenty minutes with head buried in the rear end of the car, spraying and scrubbing and mopping for all he was worth. It wasn't until he stood up and then proceeded to stagger all over the place that it became apparent that the fumes from the spirit-based cleaner had taken their effect in the enclosed space of the boot.

Guided over to a chair, with great amusement from all round, he was handed a black coffee and instructed not to move until told otherwise.

After the TR-7 rally cars had been repaired or retuned, they were taken out for an initial road run. Tim was delighted to be invited to ride along with 'Fast Eddie' who was to do the testing. A quiet, reserved man; short, slight, with occasional wisps of white hair, he appeared positively elderly.

"I climbed into the navigator's bucket seat, fitted the lap belt and we set off toward Wantage and the country lanes of the White Horse Vale. The neck-straining acceleration and engine roar was awesome, and when we hit the back roads the hedgerows became a blur, and I was thrown about violently while Eddie effortlessly put the car through its paces. I was thankful for some respite when we pulled into a lay-by. As I regained my breath Eddie turned to me: "Okay, lad. Best you put on the full safety harness now!"

On his second spell in the Design Department, Tim spent time in the terrapin hut, adjacent to the main engineering office. Alongside him were fellow apprentices Richard Woodley, Jim Halliday, Dave Seymour and Jim Stimpson.

'Jim Stim' was the loveliest old fellow you could ever wish to meet, according to Tim. Contented and happy in his work, he would spend each and every day quietly stroking away on his layout drawing whilst gently humming some tune from yesteryear.

Somehow, Richard and Tim learned that Jim was susceptible to 'earworm syndrome' and very open to subliminal suggestion. They found it most amusing to start the day by whistling or humming a pre-arranged tune and just set Jim free. A particular favourite was take the first nine notes of 'If you go down in the woods today …' whistled just once, first thing in the morning.

"We were then guaranteed to be treated to a full eight hours of *Teddy Bears' Picnic*."

Brian Courtney

Brian recalls: "I left Oxford High School at 16, in 1961, and was accepted as an apprentice at MG. They only took one apprentice every three months so over a five-year period there were only ever 20 apprentices. It was usually from these that future foremen were appointed. I could not start until January 1962, so until then for some months I became a tea-boy on the production line. Having come from a fairly sheltered background this was quite an eye-opener. I stayed there until December 1970."

During the summer when it was hot, the factory's glass roof made

Lowering the chassis from the Trim Deck where Brian spent his 'tea-boy' years.

work very difficult for the men on the lines. The tea-boys would go to an underground spring 'owned by Pavlova,' and fill tea urns with ice-cold water for the men.

"We had an apprentice association, and used to hold dances in the MG Social Club in West Saint Helen Street. This also had a rifle range. On one occasion I remember riding home on my motor bike very much the worse for wear."

Brian recalls that Personnel Manager Tony Day had charge over half a dozen MG apprentices, and he took this responsibility pretty seriously.

"Each Friday we were all to report to his office at the allotted time with our stamped time cards for inspection, and woe betide anyone whose time was not 100% compliant with assigned hours.

"As a group we were generally quite relaxed about time-keeping, as our managers and supervisors appeared to have little concern about our comings and goings, and we quickly learned it had no bearing on the wage packet at the end of the week. If we were late arriving in the morning or had enjoyed an extended lunch in the Air Balloon, it was prudent to forget to clock in and just scribble down an appropriate time on the card.

"Come the Friday appointment with Mr Day we knew that handwritten time cards just wouldn't wash. It was therefore often convenient to inadvertently forget, or be otherwise engaged at the allotted time, and just to be doubly safe, ensure that we were out of earshot of the tannoy system when the call went out 'Would … report to the Personnel Office, immediately?'

"Consequently, it is doubtful that our Personnel Manager ever succeeded in gathering all the apprentices together in one place at the same time. There was however one person who managed to achieve this.

"As we travelled through the factory, the apprentices were privy to all rumours and gossip, and naturally this information was shared. When a whisper was overheard about a forthcoming top-secret photo session in the Motorsport department, word quickly spread amongst us.

"What 'glamour-model-of-the-day' Fiona Richmond made of the gaggle of grinning young males remains a mystery, but she unknowingly achieved that feat which MG Personnel Manager Tony Day never did."

Fiona Richmond was famous, and indeed notorious, at the time, for confessing that she travelled the world 'road-testing' males of various nationalities, giving them points according to performance. Also she appeared in several risqué plays, revues, magazines and films, notably the X-rated film *Exposé* (1976) and *Fiona* (1976). No wonder the boys were grinning.

Sports

As well as cricket and rugby, every year an interdepartmental six-a-side football tournament was held, and during matches there were collections for local charities. In 1960, a team consisting of, among others, Johnny

Lay, Den Green, Tom Eales, Bob Whittington and Ray Midwinter won the football competition. MG Athletic played in the Berks and Bucks Intermediate Cup in 1979 against Drayton, wearing yellow shirts and green shorts. The full match report on this game is reproduced in the Appendix, at the end of the book. courtesy of the *Abingdon Herald*. At other times they played against such teams as Drayton, Wallingford and Milton. Table tennis was also popular, and a match report for this, too, can be found in the Appendix.

The first team became a member of the Premier Division of the Oxfordshire Senior League, and the reserve side was in the Premier Division of the North Berkshire League. They would often travel to London, Birmingham and elsewhere for matches, and this provided opportunities for people from separate work departments to get together.

Soccer Pro
Among the MG Athletic players was George Buck, an ex-professional who had earlier played for Reading FC. He decided to leave Reading when he became married and needed a regular income, which is how he came to be at MG Abingdon.

Boy Meets Girl
Lots of the boys went out with MG girls. Brian met his wife, Jo, at MG. She was an office junior, and he was a final year apprentice; they got married in 1965. Brian has a picture of his wife Jo with her friend Jenny in their office junior overalls. In 2015, they celebrated the big 50! Both big football fans, they had regularly attended the MG matches, so it was really through football that Brian and his wife first met – as did Fred and Sue Stevens.

Angling for Success
At the Social Club, as well as there being clubs for fitness, self-defence, football, table tennis, photography, rifle shooting, archery and many more, there was an MG coarse angling club at the Caldecott Road site and also, to Brian's delight, a sea-angling section. The members would travel between villages, picking up members for the trip, which was always to Mudeford near Christchurch, Hampshire, where a hired boat and bait was waiting. Brian was the only apprentice on this trip, and at £4 per week pay – always broke, so the other members used to subsidise the cost of

his trip. Brian has a photo of himself holding a skate from one trip. They used to stop halfway to the coast, and phone ahead to a café they regularly used, to order twelve breakfasts, while hoping that the sea was not going to be rough.

"Howzat!"

According to Barry Parker, the Social Club was not the only place for games. At lunchtimes a game of cricket would occasionally begin, with a tennis ball wrapped in tape to reduce the bounce. Someone would get the idea of substituting a solid ball, and this would cause it to really travel. In one game the ball smacked Barry Parker on the chin, and Ralph Owen, a white-coated inspector walking nearby shouted, "Howzat!"

At two-a-side football, the ball would sometimes be kicked over the wall of the nearby Isolation Hospital. To retrieve it someone had to climb a pile of wooden pallets, get the ball and then stand on the top of the wall to 'throw in' and restart the game.

Conshie at MG

When Brian Courtney was a tea-boy on the Trim Deck (upstairs where the car interiors were fitted before descending to the ground and becoming a 'rolling chassis'), there was one man who was fairly quiet and who was referred to as a 'conshie' (conscientious objector), but there was never any aggression towards him.

Brian recalls that for him, life at MG for a youngster was brilliant. It was a friendly relaxed place and as an apprentice he had the best of training and day-release at college. Having the Competition department on site, with all the rally cars etc., was amazing and this was at the height of the Mini and Austin-Healey 3000 successes with names like Timo Makinen, Paddy Hopkirk, Pat Moss and other MG top drivers.

Another competition success was that of Tom Haig, the Development Test Driver, apparently a member of the whisky family. He drove an MGA in the Indianopolis 500 and won its class.

Brian comments, "It was a magic environment that couldn't survive the Japanese onslaught that was over the horizon and that I was to join in 1971 when I went to work for the importers of Mazda cars, where I stayed for 30 more magic years."

Barry Dixon – at MG from 1961 to 1980
"Thanks, Dad!"

Barry's father, Eddie Dixon, had originally come from near West Hartlepool, having been a miner, and in the Thirties there was little work there. He travelled south and soon found employment in Abingdon. During the war he was in a reserved occupation so was not conscripted. His wife had been an evacuee in 1940 from the Isle of Dogs in East London and they met at the factory.

As with many other boys, Barry believed that his father's employment at MG helped Barry gain employment. Barry recalls that no tests or formal interview were needed at that time unless an apprenticeship had been applied for. Other local employment possibilities were Morlands, Pavlova or the Post Office and, at school, children were told there would be a job for life in each of them. Apart from the Post Office, none of these organisations exist now.

"Tea, Boys?"

Barry earned £1 per week for the first three years as he couldn't work on the line until he reached 18.

The day began with a 7.30am start with a 10am until 10.10 tea break. One job of the tea-boys was to take tea orders from people on the assembly lines; tea, coffee, sandwiches – and then go with the money to the canteen to fetch them. One little trick he quickly learned was that if he took the tea and coffee orders and began distributing these, if he then topped up the urns with hot water, he could sell more and make a little profit for himself. "OK, perhaps it was a little weaker than before but no one seemed to notice."

In the 1970s it seems that the canteen faced a boycott because of a price rise, but apart from that, the Hovis buns and bacon butties were 'irresistible.'

Also he got in earlier than the others in order to prepare work for the lines, eg, prepare dip-switches or headlamps so that men on piecework could get a good start. This would earn tips from the line people.

The tea-boys, even though still 14 or 15, would be used to driving the finished cars to a parking compound – this is where Barry learned to drive. On one occasion he and another boy crashed their cars together, and were suspended from driving in the factory grounds.

After three years as tea-boy he was given a choice of where to work:

Abingdon's GWR Station, c1980.

between line or stores. As there were better wages in the line, he chose that.

Work at MG then was very different from work at Cowley now, with its robot cranes and so on. At MG, production-line members had to lift car wheels up and into place, but now this is all done by machine.

Tea Mugs

A story which has appeared is that new people at MG, as well as being sent to fetch a 'long wait,' would be given a tea-mug and a hammer on beginning work. Was this only for new apprentices, or was it everyone?

Music: a Family Business

Several of the Dixon family were musically-minded. Iris, Barry's Mum, has been mentioned. Dad was a well-known pianist and played in a small band consisting of banjo, drums, piano and accordion in the MG Social Club. This was in West Saint Helen Street at one time, in part of the Clarke's building, which also served as an MG store for spare parts where Barry's father had been a chief storeman. There had been a big fire in 1944 and the place became unusable, so the club moved to Caldecott Road. The new premises consisted of a bar, ballroom, committee room, shooting range and playing fields including a tennis court. There were sometimes concert parties there in the 1950s.

A problem was that the MG company paid for the land the club was built on, while the members paid for the buildings. When the end came and the buildings were to be destroyed, the members did not make very much at all from the sale; they were knocked down and that was that. But the company could sell the land to developers and make a considerable profit, and this they did.

Abingdon GWR Station

For a while Barry worked at the MG facility at Abingdon GWR station. Completed cars were test-driven around the normal circuits, then those bound for abroad would be driven to the station and placed on flat-cars. Most were to go to the USA. Excess petrol would be drained off and batteries disconnected. They would have a sticker on the windscreen saying which US state they were bound for. He loved reading those stickers and imagining the car driving across America.

After dealing with these cars, he and friends would go over to the Railway Hotel, known (like more than one Abingdon pub), as 'Up the Steps,' and have some refreshment there.

He worked on MGA, MGB and Austin-Healey 3000 production. If there were too many of these cars, production would be stopped and they would commence work on Morris Travellers (the half-timbered ones).

When work time was over, Barry described it as a horse-race starting gate: employees on foot, on bikes and in cars would all get to the main gate, and then the gates would open, and out they would flood.

As his last job, before redundancy, he would work on MG Midgets, fixing the seats and working under the bonnet.

One perk at MG was that employees could buy lots of nuts and bolts and washers for their own cars, and slightly damaged exhausts and batteries, unsuitable for new MG cars. This was stopped eventually, possibly because some were making a small business out of it.

Cozy Dixon

Cozy began at MG in early 1976 straight from leaving school. Like so many others he started as a tea-boy, in his case in Special Tuning. When cars came in from rallies covered in mud, his job was to clean the Mini-Coopers and others down. This enabled him to meet the greats of the time such as Paddy Hopkirk. At the end of rallies, the engine would be removed for cleaning and servicing, then Cozy and others would push the car downhill, and turn left to the car-wash. A criticism Cozy has is that there is today a plaque in the gate-guards' building at the top of Colwell Drive saying: 'This is the home of MG Sports Cars' but it is in the wrong place. Where it is was formerly a security office and toilets. He feels that a plaque should be on the main police station door, which is exactly where the production line was.

On the production line they were paid by piecework, having to make about 14 cars a day. His job was to fit rear bumpers and rear brake lights.

One job he was given was to fit the gold stripe transfer on to green MGB GT V8s, rather in the way the old Airfix model transfers were put on: soak it in water and slide it into place.

Cozy notes that along the production line, the various cupboards, shelves and work-benches were covered in pin-ups which are probably less common now: particular Pirelli calendars, page 3 girls and so on.

Frank Ifield (guitar) and Cozy Dixon (drums).

When the crew had finished their quota of cars by around 2.30pm they couldn't simply go home, so sat around waiting for 5pm. Sometimes this would give time for some playful nonsense: On some occasions someone would get into a bodyshell and have a sleep. One hot afternoon, Cozy and Tim Cairns made a cardboard UFO about 2-3 feet across, taped it up and put MG dashboard lights around it and strung it up from the ceiling above the production line. Having connected the electric supply, they would make the UFO flash its lights, until the foreman came round.

Cozy's Dad was a foreman on the next line, which produced Midgets, and was there for 41 years. In a magazine article, Ernie Stone made a statement about Eddie Dixon: "Eddie was the only man who could strip an engine down to the last nut and bolt and have it listed and packaged in 2 hours for export for Australia or the USA."

Cozy once caused an accident: even now he cannot recall why he was in an MGB , but remembers the engine was going, and he tried to change gear, which he found very difficult for some reason. He managed to put it into first gear and the car shot forward and smacked into a forklift truck, which effectively wrecked the front of the MGB.

Whereas his brother Barry is a keen guitarist, Cozy was then, and still is, a noted local drummer, and at the time of leaving was in the 'Grey Seal' band, which often played at the MG Social Club in Caldecott Road, just as his father Eddie did.

On one occasion while playing at the Social Club, Eddie was playing the organ, sitting with his back to the audience on the dance floor. The crowd behind kept waving at him and trying to attract his attention because unknown to Eddie, the drummer had fallen asleep.

"I Remember You"

The time came when Cozy applied for a place in Frank Ifield's band. Frank, who recorded a number of hits in the 1960s and 1970s, such as *I Remember You*, already knew Cozy's work, and once phoned MG to ask for Cozy and to offer him a job. He got the job, and whereas he had earned £80 a week at MG, touring with Frank Ifield earned him £120. He began to tour then, supporting such performers as Ricky Valance (*Tell Laura I Love Her*) and George Hamilton IV and his son George Hamilton V – both country and western singers of some considerable fame. Once he even backed The Everly Brothers (*Wake Up Little Susie, Bye Bye Love* and many other hits).

It is all a long way from Marcham Road, but Cozy says, as many others do, that MG was a great place to work, and the people there were good to work with.

Tempest Fugit

Cozy's mother Iris performed as a singer at the social club occasionally, rendering the kind of songs Vera Lynn sang, and other popular melodies of the time. Iris also worked at MG, being employed on construction of the wings of Tempest and Typhoon aircraft.

Cozy enjoyed piecework, as you could finish at around noon. Piecework meant that if the day's allocation was 72 cars, then when these were done you could go home, often around lunchtime. He was on piecework for a time, then all went over to measured day work. This meant that a given number of cars was set, and had to be completed in a given number of hours. This apparently came about because of the introduction of time-and-motion studies, as a result of which all tasks, even in the Rectification Department, were timed. For example, and according to Brian Moylan, changing a gearbox was allowed 90 minutes, changing a radiator was 40

PASS No. A/ 2568   Badge No.

REGULATIONS

ADMIT to the Prémises of

I. This Pass is the property of The M.G. Car Co. Ltd. and must be produced upon demand made by any authorised official of the Company, at the entrance to or within the boundaries of any of the Company's properties.

THE M.G. CAR CO. LTD.
(a Protected Place as defined in Defence Regulations)

Name Mr. Dixon.

Clock No. 2527/1107.

2. Any employee of the organisation losing his/her Pass should report the matter immediately and a duplicate Pass will be issued at a charge of 1s.

National Reg. No. 10 DE. 126-6.

Department Tempest Inspection

3. This Pass is issued on the under-standing that it is to be surrendered on demand at any time by a responsible official of the Company on the instruc-tions of the constituted authority.

Sig. of Holder J. V. Dixon

G. Cooper

General Manager
for and on behalf of The M.G. Car Co. Ltd

Date of Issue 4-9-194 4

Tempest Inspection admission issued in 1944.

minutes and so on. Oddly enough, if a job took half a minute, they were allowed eight minutes, but if it took 35 minutes, they were allowed only 45 minutes, "so it all balanced out." It was similarly timed in all departments.

Experienced staff could get tasks done well within the allocated time and could then take it easy until the permitted leaving time.

On one occasion Cozy did not turn up after lunch because he had decided to go to a show in London. There were no repercussions though.

The Hudson Family

The question of whether jobs were only attainable if family members were already there is difficult to answer. In Eddie Dixon's case, he knew no-one at the time, but Barry feels his father being there helped him a good deal. There are many similar stories, supporting both sides of the argument.

MG did tend to employ multiple family members, eg, father, son, aunts and uncles, grandparents. A small number of local people believed that it was only possible to obtain a job at MG if you already had family working there, and that this was particularly true of apprenticeships. One man states that he tried MG, the Cowley factory, Morris and Pressed Steel and the only one that did not offer him a place was MG because "I knew nobody who already worked there."

Even if you did have family there this did not guarantee employment, as Mick Hudson can explain. He applied several times to MG before and after his National Service in the Royal Engineers. His father-in-law, Doug Marlow, was an Inspector, cousin Ray Hudson was on the production line, uncle Ron Wintle worked there too – his wife and Mick's father were brother and sister. Uncle Jack Booker was there, and his wife was Mick's aunt. Mick's wife worked in the Wages Office. Mick himself never did get to work there, but found employment at Cowley instead.

When possible, people tended to stop at MG, as, at the time, it offered good job security. Employees did not get pensions in those days, although management grades did – but then this was the normal situation for many working people.

Paul Murphy – President of the English Rugby Football Union

It seems that this gentleman, who became Chairman and then President of the RFU, was once employed at the MG factory and later at Cowley. His family is still resident near Abingdon. He began his apprenticeship at MG in 1968, finishing in 1972. His indentures were signed by John Thornley, the Managing Director, who had himself worked his way up from being first a service manager, then General Manager, and finally Director in 1956. Paul then went on to MG Research and Development working on vehicle safety regulations, airbags, fuel integrity and rubber bumpers.

To gain an apprenticeship (and there were about four a year), applicants would sit maths and English and other tests, to ensure that those who gained the positions were capable of benefiting from the course. Throughout their course, apprentices had to undergo annual assessment on attitude, progress, attendance etc, and some failed.

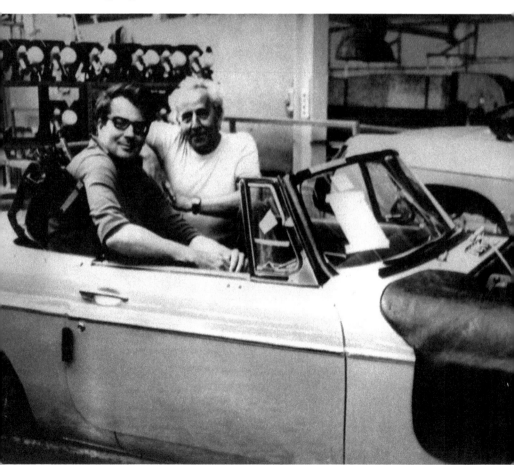

MG Production workers enjoying a little downtime in a part-built MGB.

Paul says that a favourite pastime for apprentices was using a length of brake pipe, known as bundy tubing, and a compressed air line (100psi) as a blow-pipe to fire dumdum pellets. These were made of a firm black putty used on production, and were fired at the fire-alarm bell high on the wall in the apprentice school. This was by then surrounded with black putty dots identifying the misses. A hit was rewarded with a dull 'ding.'

The MG company paid for apprentices to go on Outward Bound courses, eg, at Ullswater or Eskdale, and they were sometimes out for four days at a time. The idea behind it was to build character, team-spirit and similar things. One night Keith Faulkner accidentally put up his tent in a sheep pen. In the night, at around 3am, he and his tent were trampled on by sheep.

One Christmas Eve, while waiting to be given the go-home message in the apprentice school, a particularly obnoxious apprentice was getting on everyone's nerves. There was a gantry crane in the apprentice school, a leftover from when RAF Lancaster bomber engines (8604 of them) were built there in the war. The apprentice in question was tied in a hoist and lifted squealing up to the roof, and then the power was switched off so he could not let himself down.

Paul says: "We went home shortly after, leaving him up there. The Master of the apprentice school knew he was up there, but left him for a quarter of an hour as a lesson before letting him down."

Paul left in 1980 before the closure, and moved to Unipart Oxford to set up an engineering function to support BL's replacement parts business.

He has been awarded a British Empire Medal for services to rugby.

Keith Faulkner

Keith joined MG in 1956, and remained there until 31st of October 1980 when the works closed. The MG factory took one apprentice every three months, and four each year, and Keith was the third that year. Like others who were waiting to begin apprenticeships he filled in time as a tea-boy. He was interviewed by John Thornley ("a fantastic man") who knew everyone in the factory. Keith earned £4 a week plus tips for doing the tea, errands etc, so actually totalled up around £7 a week. Then, when his apprenticeship began, this went down to 32/6d a week. He began in the Tool Room then went to the Drawing Office, which was the normal route, spending two to three months in each then moving on. He noticed many big tank spanners in the Tool Store room, and when he asked was told; "Nothing ever gets thrown out, those are from the war!"

At one point he was offered a job in London, but chose to return to the Abingdon factory. He attended a management course at Haseley Manor in Warwick, became foreman at Abingdon in Production, and then became production supervisor, working on production planning. Later, he was placed in charge of assembly lines, mainly in the Trim department.

As supervisor, Keith saw it as sensible to run an overtime rota, to make sure all got a turn at overtime. Much of this would be for working to finish cars which had undergone shortage because of lack of supplies (for example, if a supplier had been on strike).

One of his responsibilities on the line was to deal with pay and time issues. Time-and-motion men came to time every job on the line, and disputes would arise as the assembly men wanted more time, and therefore more money, for a particular job. There would be discussion involving shop-stewards, supervisors, and the time-and-motion men. If necessary, the union convener would be called in, and then the problem would be referred to management if necessary. Usually, a compromise was arrived at. One point was that all job timings had to be coordinated so that the line could move along smoothly.

On holiday in South Africa, driving to Port Elizabeth and staying in B&Bs, the owner at one place where they decided to put up was a keen car collector. They went to their allocated room, and on a wall was a photo of Sid Enever, the MG Abingdon chief designer.

Another form of relaxation for Keith was constructing his own MGB at home. He acquired parts from damaged vehicles or by buying 'second issue' goods which had been returned to the Stores for rejection or repair.

Chapter 9

Rallying Cries

Thump!

The following tale, related by Brian Wood, concerns rallying.

"During the 1960s I was involved in rally driving, and in 1963 and 1964 I was supplied with a works-tuned Riley 1·5 by Special Tuning, Abingdon, for use in an international rally in Belgium.

"In 1965 the MG Works supplied me with a soft top MGB that had been lightly tuned. On a special race-stage in the Ardennes I was driving this car at speed down a steep hill, and half-way down there was a rail crossing. That meant that the road levelled out for about 12 feet. I was approaching this at about 60mph. My co-driver called out; 'Level crossing!' His call did not register with me, and I did not slow down. I hit the crossing and the car went up in the air, probably about four to five feet. The distance before we landed would have been even longer. Eventually we landed with a mighty thump. On impact both doors flew open and the boot shot up. I stopped and shut the doors and closed the boot and continued on my way, and successfully completed the rally.

"This stands as proof of the ruggedness and build quality of the MGB, that it could stand such punishment without any outward signs of damage."

Barry Parker tells the story that when the MG race team did well in Monte Carlo in 1964, winning the GT category, MG apprentices in Abingdon went round wearing laurel wreaths made of cabbages around their heads.

Tommy Eales

Tommy began as a tea-boy, like so many others, and learned his trade on the job. His family had moved to Abingdon as evacuees from Millwall where his father had been a docker, later getting a job on the assembly line in the MG Works.

Tom left school at 15, and began work as a shop-boy or 'gopher', being moved between departments to learn the work of the factory, starting at the Stores. His family lived in Swinburne Road at that time. When he began in the Competitions Department he knew he had found exactly what he wanted. He clearly had ability and aptitude, because Doug Watts, in charge there at the time, asked him if he would like to stay there. He worked with and learned from Den Green, and believes he owes Den a great deal. By age 20, Tom was working on his own, preparing engines, gearboxes and suspension for competition cars. He did not work on such items as wiring (all done by Lucas), on trims, or on 'tinnying' – making small fittings for the cars or finishing minor body-surface work.

Tom spent most of his time there working on rallying, and particularly recalls his adventures on the 1970 London to Mexico World Cup Rally.

This took him away from home for seven weeks, and while some said that the money was good, even if the absences were hard, Tom says that with a 94-hour week at times, it wasn't *that* good.

Mechanics took turns on these rallies, and their role was to act as a service point for their team's cars, and also act as a 'sweeper' or 'tail-end Charlie.' At one time in this rally, Tom became lost in the Andes mountains. They had flown from Santiago with a guide in a small Cessna aircraft, making their way through the mountains below the great peaks, breathing with oxygen masks. The pilot then announced that they were short on fuel and had to find a landing place. They spotted a village but landed some distance from it. The pilot went off to find it and get fuel. Meanwhile, darkness was falling, and they were in an area known for its wild pumas so they decided to walk to the village. At last they saw vehicle lights, and were picked up by a police patrol looking for 'a plane that had

come down' – theirs! They actually passed their pilot who was still walking to the village. They were helped along their way, after this, by good food and accommodation.

If they hadn't been found then, possibly they might not have been found at all. A further problem was that they had taken off in Chile and now were in Argentina, and there were political stresses between the two countries.

Other stresses were often caused by problems with Customs. With a large amount of spares to be carried, a typical Customs trick was to go over these for an hour – or sometimes up to nine hours. Often a small bribe, cigarettes for example, was the way to deal with it.

Tom recalls driving from Turkey with Bill Pike and Bob Whittington as tail-end sweepers on the London to Sydney rally, in a Wolseley 1500 known as a 'barge' (because it carried a lot, like a barge). Then through Iran and Afghanistan, giving them one night in Kabul ("the food and hotel were good.") A convoy system through the Khyber Pass, as protection from local bandits was thought necessary. Then Pakistan to Bombay (they saw the Taj Mahal) and then flew home, Tom having lost at least a stone in weight.

Lord Stokes put an end to competitions in 1970 as he had no particular interest in this area of work. As a result, Tom moved into Development, for three and a half years, testing new ideas for the engines and gearboxes, then took a foreman's job on the MGB line. He was there for three years, after which he moved to the Rectification Department as foreman, and then to Hartwell's in Park End Street, Oxford. Finally he worked in their Botley Road premises as assistant service manager.

Den Green

The *Daily Mirror* of Friday, May 29th, 1970, carries an article on the London to Mexico World Rally. Under the heading 'The Unsung Heroes Kept the Cars Going,' the writer sighs, "I certainly wish one

of them [the mechanics] lived near me!" He was writing about Dennis 'Den' Green of Abingdon who was in charge of the BL Triumph 2·5 PIs, which had previously been prepared at Abingdon for the Rally.

Den began at MG in 1957. He had worked before at City Motors Oxford as a car mechanic working on Vauxhall Veloxes for the Monte Carlo rallies. He had been a mechanic in the RAF Motor Transport Section at RAF Scampton, the 'Dambusters' airfield. The pay was not particularly good at City, and because of the closure of the Suez Canal during that crisis in 1956 there was petrol rationing. As a result there was not much work around in garages; people were just not using their cars. He attended an interview at MG, and was asked if he had ever prepared cars for rallies. As he was able to answer positively, he was finally given a job there, in the Competitions Department under Marcus Chambers and Doug Watts. He clearly did well as Den became a foreman in 1964. After the closure of the Competitions Department in 1970, senior management believing that 'Sport is a waste of time and money' Den was offered a foremanship rather than redundancy. Most of the men involved in the closure were 'old' and were happy to leave with the cash. Den worked first at piecework then on measured day work on the V8 line, producing ten cars a day. Motor sports began again in the British Leyland era, and this led to more rallying in TR7 and Dolomite Sprints in 1976.

In 1980, the Abingdon Works closure and the subsequent move of the Competition Department to Cowley meant Den was now working there. He was placed in a department checking warranty work from garages around the country. Were they charging BL too much for the work they did, or doing second-rate work? It was costing BL a fortune. Finally he left in 1987, having worked 41 years with MG in one way or another.

Den notes that John Thornley ('John Willy' or 'JWT'), founder of the MG Car Club in 1930, and MG's postwar general manager in 1952, lived at 22 Norman Avenue, Abingdon and owned plate MG 1. On the old Abingdon site there is now a Thornley Close, named in his honour.

Den loves to talk about his rallying experience around the world: Yugoslavia, South America, North America, Scandinavia, Canada, Greece, France, Spain and Belgium. He recalls some tricky driving along narrow mountain passes with a sheer drop on one side, and side-swiping a rock as he took a tight curve, resulting in some damage to the bodywork. One long trip was the London to Sydney Rally in 1968. The cars and crews drove to Bombay (Mumbai), then put the cars on a ship, the P&O liner Chusan.

From there it was ten days to Fremantle, then on to Perth, Australia, then crossing the Nullarbor Plain to the Snowy Mountains and Sydney. It is no surprise to hear that more than one marriage came to grief because of long absences abroad on rallies.

On rally in South America with, among others, Prince Michael of Kent and the footballer Jimmy Greaves ("a great character") he flew from Rio de Janeiro aiming to get to Lima, Peru. Flying in a small Cessna aircraft which was driven by a front and a rear engine, they left Santiago in a strong head wind and had to change direction simply to make headway. On the way to La Paz, capital of Bolivia, the pilot flew on his reserve tank, and when this got very low changed to the main tank. All of the men were shaken by the lack of fuel reserves, but did get to La Paz. Den recalls that they stopped near some cacti that were taller than the plane. Taking off from there the front engine started to misfire, but they were told the rear one would suffice, as it could handle flying to 10,000 feet. However the men noticed that the surrounding peaks towered to 16,000 feet. They flew through rather than over the Andes Mountains, seeing the great peaks rising far above them. In the air once again, they noticed that the oil pressure was falling rapidly. The pilot proceeded to Cuzco on one engine. On inspection after landing they saw that the underside of the plane was covered in oil. The oil-pipe had fractured. He says: "That's when I felt a long way from home."

He tells stories of equipment being impounded by Customs, of backhanders being paid. On one occasion he was confronted by armed security men. More backhanders to get the car kit back. Jimmy Cox says that there are places in the world even now to which Den cannot go and would be arrested if he did. Den caught pneumonia in Santiago, Chile, but insisted on staying at his job rather than being flown home. Regarding Mexico City he commented: "It was hard work; I don't think I could do that again." The mechanics (who prefer to be called engineers) and the drivers agreed that the rally was the best organised event they had taken part in.

People have suggested to Den that he writes down all his rallying experiences; it would certainly be a best seller among lovers of motorsport.

Bob Whittington

Bob was head prefect at Boxhill Road School and clearly impressed the headmaster with his outstanding sporting ability. When the time to leave school came round, the Head phoned up MG and asked the MG Personnel

Officer Miss Brewer to take him. This was done and no exams were needed. At that time there were no apprenticeships, but lads of the right ability did a five years skills training course around the various departments, learning the many skills and discovering their abilities and aptitudes.

He worked in the Developments department with people such as Hal Wiggins and Dave Bray, overseen by Alec Hounslow, who took his instructions from Sid Enever. This later became the Competitions department, controlled by BMC/BL, but based alongside MG Abingdon. Its

Bob Whittington.

brief was to prepare BMC/BL cars for motor sports competitions. Its first competition car was an Austin-Healey, and then came the famous Mini Coopers, which would win three Monte Carlo rallies. Later the department became BL Special Tuning during the days of the Morris Marinas, Triumph 2·5s and the Austin 1800.

Geoff Clarke tells how Alec Hounslow, manager of Developments, enjoyed a drink and a smoke. Often when representatives from Girling Brakes, Lockheed Brakes, or Champion spark-plugs came to meet with him, he would take them off to the Dog House pub for a hearty lunch.

Bob comments that he did not feel it was a job, rather it was a hobby. His main work was at rallies; East Africa, the 1968 London to Sydney Marathon, and many in Europe. In the London to Sydney Rally, they drove the cars via Kabul in Afghanistan, where they had to stay overnight and catch up on their sleep. They could not get permission to go through the Khyber Pass straight away, but had to wait until the following morning. Bob's crew then followed the rally to Rawalpindi, offering assistance as necessary. The full story is told in Brian Moylan's book *Works Rally Mechanic*.

At Bombay the cars were loaded onto a ship which would carry them to Perth, Australia, where new crews took over. Old crews and some cars were then shipped back to the UK.

In-situ repairs were a typical occurrence for MG engineers on tour with the race team.

Two major problems for rally crews were those of long absences from home, together with long preparation times getting the cars ready for the rally. Understandably, wives liked the money (one third as much again as crews would normally earn), but not the separations. Sometimes there were often only 10-14 days between periods away. The Monte Carlo Rally tended to be held around January. The Swedish rally seemed always to be held in snow and ice. The Circuit of Ireland Rally ran from Belfast around the coast and the Ring of Kerry at Easter weekend. Other rallies and races were, for example, the Scottish, The Tour de Corse, Tour of Britain, Marathon de la Route and the East African Safari. Three marriages broke up in the team, including Bob's. Later some concessions were considered where wives could perhaps spend some time during the rallies with their husbands.

In the 1970 London-Mexico World Cup Rally, held to link countries playing in the competition, and to mark the fact that the 1966 World Cup was played in London and the 1970 was to be held in Mexico, the course went through Europe, taking in Munich, Belgrade, Dubrovnik, Monza, the French Alps and on to Lisbon, Portugal. The rally was due to end five days before the first kick-off in Mexico. At Lisbon, the cars, Triumph 2·5s,

were shipped on the SS Derwent and carried to Rio de Janeiro. The rally route took them from there to Sao Paulo, across to Santiago, and over the Andes through Bolivia to La Paz and Lake Titicaca, and then to Lima. Bob's crew followed the rally crews on the route over the Andes where they needed to use lightweight oxygen masks, and to sleep where they could. According to Bob, they slept in "Some fairly ropey places."

After each rally there would be a Rally Ball and Presentation. Bob says that during the rally everyone was committed 100%, and afterwards … well, what goes on tour stays on tour. After one Monte Carlo Rally he recalls seeing the Mini designer Alec Issigonis stark naked, sitting on a rock with a flare in each hand in celebration of success.

In Monte Carlo, the French did not like dominance of the Minis and may have resorted to some tricks to prevent it. In one of them the judges decided to check headlights; the French Citroën team heard this was going to happen, and so changed their lights. The British Minis (which came 1st, 2nd and 3rd) did not, and were disqualified.

The MG Rally team, which meets every two years, is made up of drivers, navigators and engineers (not 'mechanics,' because 'engineers' also did some fabrication such as general strengthening of the rally cars, positioning skidpans on outriggers and so on; also paint spraying as the bodyshell arrived unpainted. They would then test cars on the rolling road). If there was too little time before a car was needed for a rally, it would be driven non-stop for 24 hours, with drivers replacing others at regular intervals, to get the necessary test time in.

At one point BL closed down the Competitions department as, according to Lord Stokes, it was a waste of time and money, even though BL cars came 2nd, 3rd and 4th. Bob went to work in Stores for a few months. "Yes, it was a waste of skill." Then, when competition work began again, he went into what was now Special Tuning.

This department survived the Abingdon closure as it was not part of MG but of BL, and the Department was moved to the BL works at Cowley.

Bob's son Darren fondly recalls being taken to an MG Social Club Christmas party in 1973, and being bounced up and down on the knee of no other than the great driver Paddy Hopkirk.

Doug Hamblin

Jean Hamblin, the wife of Doug Hamblin, was good enough to call in response to an advertisement in the *Oxford Mail*, asking for the reminiscences of ex-MG people, in order to tell her husband's story.

Doug, who lived in East Hanney, had worked at MG before his national service, and then again from 1949 to 1964. He worked on the rallies at MG, in the Competition department.

On 19th January, 1964, Doug was on his way to Southend airport to join the MG team in France for the Monte Carlo Rally, when he was killed in a car crash. The car he was in was being driven by Robin Vokins of Milton, and they collided with a car driven by a man from Chislehurst, Kent, on an icy patch of road near Remenham, Berkshire. To this day his wife, Jean, has not been able to visit the site of the crash.

Den Green and Doug Hamblin were good friends. Recently, Den was given Jean's phone number, so they are now in regular contact with each other and can discuss old times.

Chapter 10

Customers and Visitors

Here is a selection of miscellaneous items, which are intended to show other sides of life at MG, the involvement of media, of families and interest from customers abroad.

The Italian Job

Peter Thouless says that the Minis used in *The Italian Job* film were built in the Competitions Department, and the Works' pantechnicon was resprayed and used in the film.

Inside the BL Competitions Department at MG.

MG TV!

The BBC children's programme *Blue Peter* visited the factory in the early 1970s to make a film featuring Valerie Singleton, one of the presenters of the programme. The story goes that she was very bad tempered, and once, when offered a chair rather than have to sit on the floor, she shouted; "If I want a chair, I'll ask for one!"

There was once a visit by some police officers, and as they walked round enjoying their tour, all the men on the line began whistling *Johnny Todd*, the theme tune from the TV police programme *Z-Cars*.

Noel Edmonds visited the Works in 1971 for publicity reasons. Fred Stevens was in the formal photograph. Philip Bolton thinks Edmonds may have purchased an MGB during his visit.

Christmas

Every Christmas on the MG line they would decorate the line, and have a full-size Father Christmas; a wiper motor was used to make his arm wave, and flashing lights were fixed in the eyes and in the nose.

There are photographs of the assembly lines decorated in home-made bunting, and of the vehicles being lowered through them from the upper floor. It seems that the decorations were made in lunchtimes and breaks, and no time was lost from vehicle production.

The workforce's under-12 children had a Christmas party in the Corn Exchange, paid for by the factory and with donations from the workforce.

Every year there was a big Christmas raffle with 'thousands' of prizes.

Keith recalls that one year he spent £20 (the equivalent of about £50 today) on tickets – and only won a Dundee cake.

On the final day of production before Christmas they would go round with collection buckets for local charities.

American Tours

Once a week, possibly on a Thursday, some of the men would have regular factory tours for American MG owners.

Barrie Robinson – Some Thoughts From Canada

Barrie Robinson sent a message from Canada, telling of his experiences as a satisfied, and very technically aware, MG customer.

"My father bought me a brand new MG TD when I was in Malaya. I was working for a British import company. I 'raced' it and loved it but changed to a TR2 and beat-up Jaguars. Many years later I was sent from the UK as a computer sales engineer to Montreal – 'just for a year' – and have been in Canada ever since. I collected a few cars, two of which were MGBs. I then built an MGB GT V8 which I have run for many years – a marvellous machine. I am very experienced in the subject of British dumb marketing and the GT V8 was one of them. BL, in their mighty dumbness, brought out successors of the MGB only to be slaughtered by the Miata and others. Why BL loaded the MGB with expensive sound, leather and other expensive do-dads when it was completely contrary to MG mystique is beyond belief. The MG sales dried up because BL was not firing on all cylinders, and while purchasers of the later MG variants liked them, the US market had moved on … and thus Miata. Even now Brit companies are missing out on the huge MG-following in the US – and 'Chinese globular pseudo-MG tubs are not attractive.'

"It surprises me that someone has not streamlined the GT shell, dropped in a decent engine, better suspension and left all the do-dads off so it was cheap. The engine should be the Rover V8 (improved of course) as it still beats the current lumps. My MGB GT V8 has a mildly modified Rover V8 of course, and it goes like stink with 38 mpg!!

"I understand that the MGB (GT?) was the first car to be crash tested and came out with flying colours – is this correct?"

(Author's note – Apparently this was indeed the case. There was a crash facility in the Abingdon Works, and cars would be driven fast into a concrete slab to check weak points, an idea first dreamed up at the MG Works. All this was to satisfy the US market and its many regulations.)

Building a V8

"I had a fantastic experience from building my MGB GT V8 to factory specs. Because I upped the Rover engine to over 200bhp it created more heat and getting over that is a book in itself! I now wrestle with the expected heat problem with my 1957 Aston Martin which I am restoring. British cars were built for British climates so one has to up the ante for North America. A good way to start is using an aluminium radiator (actually it is the second best thing to do). The Aston radiator is a typical Aston design – very complex!

"My V8 is now sitting out the winter in a nice dry barn as I do not drive it while salt is on the road. The Canadians and Americans have a love of salting roads – probably subsidised by the body repair industry!"

Chapter 11

A Great Future? Maybe.

On 3rd April 1980, seven months before the MG Works closure, the *Herald* newspaper carried a front page article on MG. It disclosed with great confidence that a new model MG would be on the road by 1983. Alan Curtis, the head of MG did not confirm this – he was 'tight-lipped' on the matter, but did state; "I can confirm nothing. There are ideas."

In an August 1979 issue of the *Abingdon Herald*, Peter Frearson, the Abingdon plant director, announced there would be a carnival to celebrate the 50th year of MG in Abingdon – a Golden Jubilee would be held between 1st and 8th of September, when around 75 floats, eight bands, and examples of cars made at MG would take part in a procession. There would be a football match between Abingdon Town FC and the MG Social and Athletic Club, fireworks, and a grand jubilee dance. The Oxfordshire Pearly King would make an appearance, as would the RAF Robins parachute team. There was much more, too. Large, full-page notices appeared in the local press. The third largest air balloon ever flown in England would be there, with a huge MG logo emblazoned upon it.

Early in 1979 suspicions were raised, casting doubts on the company's future. Employees knew something was going on when Sir Michael Edwards visited the factory, but didn't feel comfortable when with the men, and didn't spend time talking with them. It all left an unsettling sense of nagging insecurity.

The MG 50th Jubilee

At the jubilee in August the whole town was toasting the next 50 years of MG. One 'Jubilee Midget' was made, painted British Leyland green, and was won in a draw by Jim Fletcher – who could not drive, so the car fell into the hands of his daughter. Jim had worked on motor torpedo boats in the war, and, on the day MG closed, fell down the stairs from the canteen.

Phil Bolton obtained one of only 50 pewter tankards inscribed with MGB and logo (No 1963). Den Green also possesses one.

As well as the tankards, a number of gold-coloured MGBs were produced for the Jubilee. One of the last of these is on display in the Gallery of Abingdon County Hall Museum, together with a video of how it came to be placed up there on the first floor.

Old Speckled Hen

'Old Speckled Hen' beer had been specially brewed for the 50th Jubilee. It was named after a car made 50 years before, which had got its name from

the golden speckled cellulose fabric stretched over its wooden frame. The car's original formal name was the MG Featherweight Fabric Saloon, but it was never actually made in Abingdon. Originally planned to be brewed only for six months, the beer came in half pint bottles, not draught. There was a rumour for some time that the first one was poured as draught in the MG Social Club, but Glyn Walters assures me that it was not, and could not have been; there was no such draught at that time. It is, of course, still available today.

The Willis Hexagon

Mr Ron Willis of the Rectification department was a gifted amateur artist. He created a hexagon about three feet across, in which he painted a small picture of every model MG car the factory had ever made between 1929 and 1979. This is now on the wall in the Douglas Mickel Room at the MG Car Club.

On the day of the Jubilee, held on the MG sports field on Caldecott Road, there was, fortunately, good weather. As well as all the other fun and games, there was a pram race through town with 25 teams, each pram crewed by 3-4 people (men or women). These came from local pubs, for example, Nag's Head ladies, White Horse, Air Balloon, Blue Boar. There was also the MG Marauders team. The team from the Broad Face won. The idea was that one crew member would sit in the pram, and be pushed by the others. They would have to stop at 18 pubs, have a drink, change the person in the pram and run on to the next one. Visited drinking establishments included the Conservative Club, Air Balloon, Mr Warwick's, Boar, Swan, and the Anchor. The race ended at the MG sports ground in Caldecott Road.

MG Jubilee Beauty Queen

For some years the MG Social Club had run an annual Miss MG beauty queen contest, some of the winners being Sue Holland, Sandra Kinchen (who had several family members at the works), and Shirley Collins. In 1979, Miss Kim Neal, 18, of Caldecott Road, was chosen as 'Miss MG Jubilee Queen.' She had fought off competition from 19 others for the position. Runner-up was Mariena Rowland of Palmer Close. The competition had been held at the Sports and Social Club in June and on the first Saturday of the carnival, it was Kim who put a match to the fireworks display there.

At the MG 50th Jubilee, Fred Stevens helped to make a big cardboard 'cake' which was bolted on to a Mini – a white tiered cake with pink drinking cup decorations, all constructed in normal working hours, according to Fred. Arthur Hedges drove the Mini inside it. A keen footballer, Arthur was also heavily involved in organising the Saxton Rovers FC youth team, and this may have affected his health later.

An interesting point is that on the day of the Jubilee, the invited sales force of 150 Americans and their wives found that nothing was planned for when the afternoon events finished, until a civic reception in the evening at the Council Chamber. In fact, it had been decided that individual employees were supposed to take an American (plus wife) into their home and offer entertainment, freshening-up facilities, and so on, before they went to hear the council's speeches. The MG people actually took their charges off to 'a good old-fashioned English pub,' which turned out to be 'The Vine' at Cumnor.

None of the guests wanted to leave once settled in there, but the council arranged for the MG people also to be given tickets for the evening events, and so off they all went. Honour was satisfied.

The End

The same year (1980) the *Abingdon Herald* carried the following headline: 'Abingdon Jubilee Turns Sour – The Car BL Can't Afford to Sell.' The claim was that MG had become a victim of the high rate of exchange between

The MG at 50 'cake' during the 50th anniversary parade celebrations.

the US dollar and the British pound. The American west coast was MG's biggest US market, but the fall in profit margins made such sales not worth the factory's while.

Around this time 450 of the 1100 employees were laid off because of a strike that in fact did not touch Abingdon. However, it did lead to parts shortages, especially of axles.

Redundancies were announced days after the 50th Jubilee of MG, and very soon after the workforce had been told they were doing a great job by Deputy Director Ray Horrocks in a rousing speech: "What a fantastic future you all have."

Everyone Shocked

The management – and *The Oxford Times* and Radio Oxford – made the redundancy announcement on the following Monday.

The factory closure shocked everyone. Some described Abingdon as 'a

town in mourning' because some families with several at the Works now had several incomes snatched away. Many would now be out of work at least for a while. Apparently, it was the same overall feeling when Pavlova, always referred to as the 'Pav', finally closed in 1993, and also when Morland's Brewery closed in 2000.

In October 1980, there was a big march in London to demonstrate against the closure of MG Abingdon, and Jimmy Cox was close to the front. There is a video of the march on YouTube.

In August 1980, the MG Owners' Club organised a convoy of vehicles at walking pace through parts of Oxford, the Abingdon Road and Abingdon with the aim of getting jobs for MG employees, and leaflets were handed out. The campaign had little success.

Locals say that when they were at the point of leaving school as youngsters, they were always told "If you get a job at Morland's, Pavlova or MG, you'll have a job for life." Now they are all closed down.

On the lighter side, much employment was created when Milton Trading Estate was expanded in the year 2000, and it now has 250 organisations and employs 7500 people. Abingdon's unemployment rate is now less than the national average, at about 1.2%.

Nevertheless, at the time, it is said that grown men were in tears, especially the older ones who feared they would find no further work locally.

The MG closure also shook visiting US business people. These were men who sold MGs in the United States, and had come to Abingdon to join in the 50th Jubilee celebrations. Immediately after this came the closure announcement, and the feeling was that any amount of MG cars could still be sold in the States, so why close? They were very dismayed and angry. This was not helped by the knowledge that TR-7s and Jaguars were not good sellers in the United States.

The MG Diaspora

There were nearly 800 redundancies; the *Abingdon Herald* gives the figure 720, who were put on a two-day work system and given 90-day notices of redundancy. Another 100 who worked at BL's Cowley plant were put on other employment.

Once redundancies were announced (which were due to take place on Friday, October 24th 1980), MG planned a course on being self-employed. The idea was to help the men use their money wisely. They would be receiving amounts of between £1500 and £10,000, depending on average weekly pay and length of service.

Some employees then found work in MFI in Oxford, or at the Morris Cowley Works or Esso Research, working on engine testing. Others found work at the developing Milton Trading Estate. Others of course took retirement.

Self-Employment

Personnel Officer Tony Day commented: "A fair number have intimated to us that they are interested in seeking self-employment, and the last thing we want is for them to be separated from their money in a short time. This can easily happen when running your own business."

He said that about 50 workers had shown an interest in the five-day course, which was to run in conjunction with the Abingdon College of Further Education. It would begin on 29th of September and continue when the factory had shut down.

"Our men have had a degree of independence, and if they cannot work at MG they would prefer to work for themselves." They would probably start businesses in window-cleaning, car maintenance or electrical work. One became a turf-accountant.

The Head of Business at the college said that the main problem would be keeping capital intact. Legal matters would be explained, and such people as bank managers and insurance representatives would speak on the course.

Mr Day commented: "You don't think what to do with £5,000 until the cheque is in your hand, and we are trying to get them to think about it now."

Ex-employees say today that about 90% of them were taken on at Cowley, in an agreement between Cowley and the relevant trade union, the General and Municipal Workers' Union.

Sue Steven's cousin, Peter, was not very able. His little MG job was a lifeline, hanging fascia panels on hooks which took them into a reservoir of toxic liquid – "you could smell him coming home into the house." This work was his whole life. He became very depressed when redundancy took effect. Finally he became very ill and died of a stroke. His family wondered: was it brought about by continued unprotected exposure to the toxic liquid ?

Several did take re-training and became self-employed; Andy Glass (shop-boy and line-fitter) went into the glazing business, Gary Bramley became a self-employed builder. Alan Evans became a body shop owner on Lodge Hill, Abingdon, Graham Berry from the assembly line began Lottery Windows, while Mike Torevell of the Drawing Office went to work with Lotus of Norwich.

It seems that generally, unemployment in town was not too badly affected.

Gunners Fired

One long-serving member of staff was 'Uncle Stan' Bradford, who, before working at MG for 35 years, had been a Warrant Officer in the RAF, serving as a mid-upper gunner in Lancaster bombers flying from RAF Scampton in Lincolnshire. He was awarded the Distinguished Flying Medal, having completed 79 missions and shooting down six enemy aircraft over Germany, two of them on one flight. It is of interest that quite possibly the engines of his aircraft had been made in the Abingdon Works.

Stan had worked on at least one rally, the London to Sydney, where he drove or crewed one of the Princess 'barges.' He now has a bottled beer named after him; 'Gunner's Gold,' produced at the Abingdon 'Loose Cannon' brewery.

As well as Stan Bradford, Dick Seddon was also a Lancaster bomber gunner – he became an assembly line foreman at MG.

Closing of MG – Why?

A problem was that MG was gradually making less and less money on each car, particularly as the US/UK exchange rate became increasingly disadvantageous to British manufacturers exporting to the US. Another factor was that BL was not prepared to go to the expense of replacing the dies and presses which were reaching the end of their useful lives. According to Vito it got so bad that often one side of the car was actually shorter than the other, because of uneven wear on the machinery. As a result, under Sir Michael Edwards, all investment went into the TR7 because there was little point in two separate cars, the MGB and TR7, competing for the same segment of the market. TR-7s were built at Longbridge, then Speke, Liverpool, but apparently were not a success, as the Americans did not want them. In fact for two years it was voted the worst car imported into USA.

A former WWII Gunner, Dick Seddon (third from left) and others from MG.

Another reason related by Keith Faulkner, was that BL sold off the Abingdon factory because, having the freehold, it was the only one they could sell; they leased all the others. Interestingly, Aston Martin wanted to buy the Works, but British Leyland would not let them buy the MG marque – they wanted to use it themselves, for example on the MG Metro, Maestro and others – all badged cars. So Aston Martin failed to buy it.

The reasons for closing remained ambiguous to employees. When asked how people felt at having a 50th Jubilee in 1979, then days later being made redundant, Iris Dixon says she knows that two men from Drayton became very depressed and ill indeed. No doubt there were others.

Dutchy's Opinion

Frank Holland believed that one cause of closure was that the unions in the Works had gained too much power. One example was that piecework was replaced by Measured Day Work. This was intended to give more time for completion of the daily number of vehicles, but it all went wrong when the assembly staff finished just as they had before, and spent two or three hours just sitting around doing very little, before they could go home. The unions demanded, and got, a half-hour break at the end of work before they would allow men to begin overtime. He described the management at MG as 'chaotic' towards the end. Indeed he said there was 'NO' real management.

The hollow shell of the former works, stripped of all its parts, machinery, and anything of use.

Ill-Feeling at Cowley

At Cowley, Pete Jeffries met some ill-feeling when he first went there after MG. He realised that the men there were unhappy having 'outsiders' take jobs they perhaps wanted themselves. But eventually he felt that he fitted in.

Pete had moved to Cowley as electrician foreman, and while he was there an unusual incident occurred. He was thinking of applying for a supervisory post which was advertised in the *Herald*, and felt that if he didn't get it he wanted to leave. He phoned the number given in the *Herald*, but this was apparently the wrong one. It was in fact the number of Pete's supervisor, and the man's wife answered. Fortunately it all ended happily, and Pete indeed became a supervisor at Cowley, with four or five foremen under him (electrical and mechanical, tool-room, cleansing, and plant-attendance). This represented about 80 men. He worked from 1980 until 2000.

When the MG social club ground was sold off, all the members got a share of about £2000 each.

Aunt Sally Kit

A final story – but the teller has asked to remain anonymous. Once the Club was sold off, bits and pieces remained. Among these was the Aunt Sally shed and its equipment (a very popular outdoor game in parts of South East England). A person was driving past in his van and saw this equipment standing apparently unwanted and ready to be burned. He picked them up and put them in his van. He then drove off and donated them to the landlord of the Crown pub in Ock Street, Abingdon. The pub has since closed, but perhaps somewhere the MG Aunt Sally pieces are still being used to this day.

Chapter 12

Conclusion

FREEHOLD INDUSTRIAL PROPERTY
APPROX
410,000 SQ.FT.
ON 42 ACRES

FOR SAL

 Hillier Park

May and Ro

77 Grosvenor Street London W1

01·629 766

A single, simple message comes through from these reminiscences; the great majority of those who worked at the Abingdon factory were happy to do so, and many stated that a high degree of pride in a great product also added to their deep sense of job satisfaction.

Several people mention the special 'family feeling' they experienced there and this was quite appropriate as many local families could show that two, or sometimes even four or five members, male and female, were employed there.

The memories of those who have contributed have to some small extent revived what could almost have been described as the beating heart of Abingdon. Through its highly successful cars and the company's success in rallies and in motorsport generally, the influence of the town reached to all parts of the United Kingdom and of Europe, and far out across the world, from the deserts of Australia to the great peaks of the Andes.

Perhaps the company's greatest celebration was to be seen in the 50th Anniversary Jubilee in 1979. A week of festivities with the huge hot-air balloon, the parades, MG's Jubilee Beauty Queen, novelty races, and a large contingent of sales-people from the United States, led the towns-people to believe that their company had a great future to look forward to.

They were encouraged in this view by spokespeople from the management, who told them that new models of car were being planned, requiring a larger workforce.

A sense of melancholy exists in these past pages. It can truly be said that grown men wept when, a few brief days after the Jubilee, the announcement was made that the Works was to close. A sense of profound shock rippled through the town, and anger turned on the management who, it was felt, must have known of this even as they promised a secure future. Some of the reasons for closure are described in the text: exchange rates between the pound and US dollar, costs of re-tooling, and rationalisation of inventories by British Leyland.

However, even now, 36 years after the closure, those I have spoken with have what can only be described as a lingering passion for their work at MG. They hold regular reunions, which are always well attended, and the MG Car Club is still thriving.

The point has been mentioned here that, just outside Abingdon, MGs are even today being developed, as they are by a Chinese manufacturer. The marque will continue to exist for a long time yet.

149

Acknowledgements

The author would like to thank the following for their support in compiling, editing and publishing this unique recollection of stories, anecdotes, images and other contributions.

Abingdon County Hall Museum
Stuart Jackson
The British Motor Heritage
Company, Witney
Peter Jeffries
MG Car Club, Abingdon
Bob Matthews
Tony Barrett
Dave Mildenhall
Roy 'Titch' Belcher
Peter Neal – MGCC
Antony Binnington
Glyn Northing (proof-reading)
Philip Bolton
Vito Orlando
Tim Cairns
Steve Palmer
Geoff Clarke
Barry Parker
Rod Clewley
Derek Powell
Brian Courtney
Barrie Robinson

Jimmy Cox
Sue and Fred Stevens
Tim Davies
Brian and Topsy Salsbury
Barry Dixon
Cozy Dixon
John Struggles
Iris Dixon née Taphouse
Peter Thouless
Tommy Eales
Tony Thouless
Keith Faulkner
Glyn Walters
Heather Grant
Bob Whittington
Irene Grant née Bennett
Darren Whittington
Den Green
Brian Wood
Jean Hamblin
Mickey Haynes
Nigel Hawkins

Pictures and resources

The author thanks Abingdon County Hall Museum for providing the time and resources, both textual and pictorial, in completing this volume and for permitting the reproduction of such content.

The following images have also been included by kind permission:
MG marque logo (black and white), front cover, British Motor Heritage Centre, Gaydon, United Kingdom
MG Offices, p.52-53, MG Car Club, Abingdon, United Kingdom

Bibliography

North Berkshire Herald and *Abingdon Herald*, various 1929-1980.
Brian Moylan, *MG's Abingdon Factory*, Veloce Publishing, 2007.
Brian Moylan, *Works Rally Mechanic*, Veloce Publishing, 1998.
George Propert, *MG War Time Activities* – edited by Colin Grant, MG Car Club.
Brian Robins, *The Great Rally*, IPC Magazines, 1970.
Graham Robson, *The Daily Mirror 1970 World Cup Rally*, Veloce Publishing, 2010.
Abingdon County Hall Museum, *Abingdon Remembered* – Oral History Project, 2010.
Frank Holland, *Lucky Dutch – The Life Story of Frank Holland, a Very Ordinary Man* – self-published.
Don Hayter, *Don Hayter's MGB Story*, Veloce Publishing, 2012.

Appendix: MG Sports in the News

The following snippets of text, taken from local newspapers, recount just a few of the many sporting activities in which teams from the MG Works were involved.

MG Athletic v Marston United – 20th January 1972
MG Athletic 3 – Marston United 1

MG's recent improved form, which had seen them gain 6 points from the four games, continued on Saturday when they defeated Marston United 3-1 in a Hellenic League Division 1A match at Abingdon. For the first 15 minutes Marston attacked strongly, playing good close possession football and they were rewarded with a penalty in the 14th minute when BUTLER brought down one of their players. However the resultant kick was hammered against the crossbar and MG breathed again.

In fact it was then the MG side who took control, Marston seeming to lose confidence and when the visitor's right winger attempted to clear the ball across the face of his own goal, GEORGE BUCK intercepted and the rebound was driven home by FRANK ALLEN from 20 yards.

Just before the interval, MATTHEWS cleared the ball from the centre circle and ALLEN seized upon a chance created by hesitation in the Marston defence to score again. ALLEN scored the third goal as MG increased their lead after the break. This goal was created after a ball from BRAMLEY was left by PALMER and ALLEN used the space created, to net.

Marston, not to be outdone, hit back with a fine goal from a fierce shot by their left half after the MG defence had half-heartedly cleared.

The motormen scored again through GEORGE BUCK but the goal was disallowed because WESTON had wandered into an offside position.

(Courtesy of *North Berks Herald*)

MG Athletic v Drayton – Berks and Bucks Intermediate Cup
October 1979
Drayton 0 – MG Athletic 1

If only corners counted Drayton would have won their home Berks and Bucks Intermediate Cup against MG Athletic in a canter, but instead, despite creating enough chances to have nullified ANDY PARRY'S 17th minute goal, they were guilty of their own inability to finish, and their defeat was of their own making.

The tie as it gained some momentum produced some delightful midfield play. The MG side were well served by ALAN BAYLISS and the industrious and hard-working RONNIE MACKAY, whilst the ever present Mel James was a tower of strength constantly providing a stream of crosses into the box for Drayton. Pete Fuller, who had a fine game in midweek for the Berks and Bucks Junior side, gave an impressive display and was desperately unlucky not to be awarded a penalty in the second half. Nevertheless it was the defences on both sides who took the honours.

As early as the fourth minute the North Berks side let slip a fine opportunity, a splendidly struck flag kick by Graham Marks found Drayton's Alie Dewe by the far post who calmly nodded the ball back into the goal-mouth but no home player was able to turn the ball over the line.

In MG's first threat MICKY WOODRUFF got in a firmly struck shot but Ian Gordon , who returned to the home side after several weeks out through a badly cut hand, saved in confident style.

Back came Drayton and a free kick firmly hit by Marks saw the Works keeper MICKY KING, who played a key role in his side's narrow victory, turn the ball around the post for a corner. With the game in its 15th minute the MG Athletic went extremely close when BAYLISS worked the ball down the left, chipped a perfect centre for WOODRUFF to power fractionally wide of the Drayton upright. Minutes later PARRY was only inches away with a bullet-like header, but within seconds he put the Works side ahead when for once there was a misunderstanding between the home defence and the keeper. Gordon called for the ball and the home defence allowed it to go through but slight indecision by the keeper was seized on by the MG Athletic striker who powered the ball home.

With the tie delicately poised the

final 15 minutes were really hectic. Drayton appealed strongly when Fuller was brought down in the box and later Brian Smith appeared to have been hampered by the MG Athletic keeper when in a good position to score.

The closing minutes saw MG Athletic renew their efforts and a second goal looked very much on the cards when they won their first corner of the match but Parry's goal shot was well saved by Gordon.

(Courtesy of *Abingdon Herald*)

Didcot and District Table Tennis, Division 3 – October 1978

In Division 3, MG C gave AERE G a bit of a fright when they went 2-0 up and continued to hold the upper hand until the final singles and the doubles. MG's DAVID GRAY obtained a maximum but was made to battle against John Long having to go to three. Long also took DILL to three. Paul Stratton gained some comfort in beating BUCKNER after losing to DILL 21-14, 19-21, 19-21. Alan Matthews also had a close match against DILL, winning 16-21, 21-19, 21-19, and partnered Long to win the doubles and gain a draw.

(Courtesy of *Abingdon Herald*)

In Memoriam

It is with great sadness that during the compilation of this book I learned of the passing of Brian Moylan (1928-2017).

He was a long-serving member of the MG Car Company, President of the MG Abingdon Works Centre, and author of several excellent books on the marque and the Abingdon factory, including *Works Rally Mechanic, Anatomy of the Works Minis,* and *MG's Abingdon Factory.*

Brian's knowledge, advice and donations were integral to completing the permanent MG displays at Abingdon County Hall Museum in 2012.

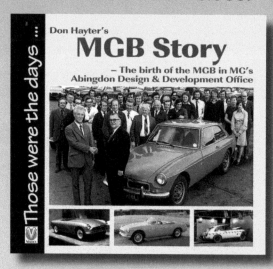

This invaluable book provides a step-by-step introduction to basic car electrical theory, and its explanation of how each MGB system works, the clear and simple colour diagrams and easy fault finding guides will make everyone an expert.

ISBN: 978-1-787110-52-6
Paperback • 27x20.7cm
192 pages • 400 pictures

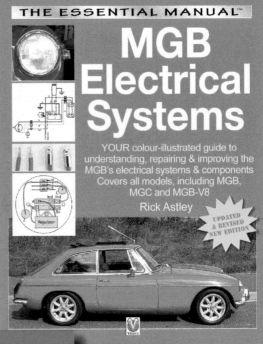

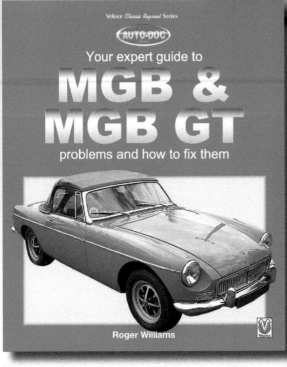

All models of car have their own common faults and foibles as well as the general ills that can afflict all cars. This book represents the collected knowledge of many MGB experts and allows problems to be identified and assessed quickly, and then to be dealt with in the most appropriate way.

ISBN: 978-1-787110-46-5
Paperback • 25x20.7cm 176 pages • fully illustrated

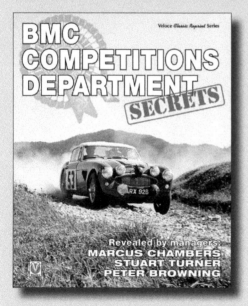

Index

159